THE HOLY CENTER

THE HOLY CENTER
A Biblical Path to the Presence Within

Dorothea Harvey

Chrysalis Books

copyright © 2005, 2ⁿᵈ edition, by Dorothea Harvey

First printing 1983

Library of Congress Catalog Card Number: 83-060258

Library of Congress Cataloging-in-Publication Data

Harvey, Dorothea
      The holy center : a biblical path to the Presence within
Dorothea Harvey. —2ⁿᵈ ed.
     p. cm.
ISBN 0-87785-172-7
1. Sacrifice in the Bible—Meditations. 2. Worship in the Bible—Meditations. 3. Tabernacle—Meditations. 4. Bible. O.T. Exodus—Meditations. 5. Bible. O.T. Leviticus—Meditations. 6. New Jerusalem Church—Prayer-books and devotions—English. I. Title.
BS 1245. 6. S2H37 2005

222' . 12064—dc 22   2004029761

Credits: The Scripture quotations contained herein are from the New Revised Standard Version Bible, copyright © 1989 by the Division of Christian Education of the National Council of the Churches of Christ in the U.S.A., and are used by permission. All rights reserved.

Designed and typeset by Karen Connor

Set in Jansen

Chrysalis Books is an imprint of the Swedenborg Foundation, Inc. For more information, contact:

      Chrysalis Books
      Swedenborg Foundation
      320 North Church Street
      West Chester, PA 19380
      800-355-3222
           or
      visit us at www.swedenborg.com.

• CONTENTS •

The tabernacle was for Israel the sign of God's intent to dwell with its people, the place of God's continuing Presence in their midst. The story of the tabernacle and of the worship and the sacrifices associated with it might seem to be the ancient history of some remote tribe, except for one thing: the story consists largely of directions for the people's use of the tabernacle, that is, their approach to the Presence, their worship, and their living in its light. And when we study the directions, we find ourselves in the Presence, hearing God's Word to us about our approach to the Lord, our doubts and confusions as we try to bring our lives toward God's light to worship.

I began my study of this part of the Bible with hesitation. But what I found was a direct and sensitive response to my inner need as the words of the Bible became God's Word to me. And I learned that I was not alone in my confusions. Others, from ancient Israel on, had suffered them before me, but had found their way to God's continuing and supporting Presence notwithstanding. My first assumption in this writing is, then, that God's Word is present in the

Bible and speaks to us in the most practical ways of the issues of our inner lives. If we need help in our approach to finding God, these chapters of the Bible are for us.

My second assumption is that the images in the Bible are words of power. "The LORD is my shepherd" needs no defence or explanation. The image itself speaks, with new power each time we hear it, if we let ourselves respond to it at all. The images relating to God in the end of the book of Isaiah (40:11) have an equal immediate power. God is the ruler coming with strength who

> . . . will feed his flock like a shepherd;
> he will gather the lambs in his arms,
> and carry them in his bosom,
> and gently lead the mother sheep.

God relates to Israel as a mother who cannot

> . . . forget her nursing child,
> or show no compassion for the child of her
> womb. (Is. 49:15)

God is the hero of the creation warfare who pierced the chaos dragon of the universe to make a cosmos (51:9). God, the Maker of Israel, is the husband who will have compassion on his briefly forsaken wife (54:6). God is the warrior putting on righteousness as a breastplate (59:17), glory rising as light upon his people (60:2). God will rejoice over Israel "as the bridegroom rejoices over the bride" (62:5). God is "our Father," "our potter" for us the clay (64:3). And "as a mother comforts her child," so Israel will be comforted by God like a child held in her lap (66:12–13). This end of the Book of Isaiah proclaims once and for all the one God of all history and all creation, but the language is not our labored writing of sentences about God's omnipotence and omniscience. The language of the Bible is that of concrete, vivid images to which we must respond, with feeling and living as well as thought, in order to know their meaning and their power.

Every reader of the Bible has recognized this power of image in the psalms and in the prophets. I have found in these chapters describing the worship associated with the tabernacle the same power of image. This, I believe, is the language of the Bible as a whole, its history and religious practices, as well as its poetry and prophecy. Israel had a political life in this world, and her history as recorded in the Bible may be studied and checked for literal accuracy in the light of the history and culture of other ancient peoples. But the history of Israel recorded in the Bible is also, I believe, the history of the inner life and growth of every human being. My intention in this work is to look at the biblical directions for the tabernacle and the worship associated with it as true history to be studied with all the help of the critical understanding of its original cultural setting that I can find, and at the same time as true image to which I must respond to hear God's Word to me.

This approach is not new. It is based on an earlier study of the tabernacle, *The Jewish Sacrifices*, by the Reverend John Worcester (1834–1900), a minister who based his work on the findings of the eighteenth-century scientist and theologian Emanuel Swedenborg (1688–1772). Worcester's work, first published in Boston in 1902, was part of a significant influence of Swedenborg in the thinking of the time. William James (1842–1910) was doing his pioneer work in psychology and religion. Elwood Worcester (1862–1940) and others were active in the Emanuel Movement to bring the insights of religion, psychology, and medicine together to enhance the lives of people. Swedenborgians, with their commitment to the Bible as God's Word, their equally strong sense of the power of symbol, and their acceptance of science as a natural ally of religion, were well suited to such endeavors. In 1909, the visit of Sigmund Freud (1856–1939) and Carl Jung (1875–1961) to this country eclipsed these Swedenborgian efforts, but, of course, contributed enormously to popular awareness of spiritual-psychological reality and to serious, continued interest in the relationship of religion, psychology, and spiritual growth.

The present work is the result of my engagement in John Worcester's original study of the tabernacle and its sacrifices, to make it available in new and modern form. It is offered with appreciation of Worcester's and Swedenborg's insights, and with thanks to the Swedenborg Foundation for suggesting the project.

THE HOLY CENTER

1

The LORD said to Moses: Tell the Israelites to take for me an offering; from all whose hearts prompt them to give you shall receive the offering for me. This is the offering that you shall receive from them: gold, silver, and bronze, blue, purple, and crimson yarns and fine linen, goats' hair, tanned rams' skins, fine leather, acacia wood, oil for the lamps, spices for the anointing oil and for the fragrant incense, onyx stones and gems to be set in the ephod and for the breastpiece. And have them make me a sanctuary, so that I may dwell among them. In accordance with all that I show you concerning the pattern of the tabernacle and of all its furniture, so you shall make it.

When the people of Israel were in search of their identity and sense of purpose in the world, they looked to their origins, to the deliverance from Egypt, the making of covenant, the encounter with the Presence of God in its symbols of fire and cloud on

Sinai. They looked to those momentous events in history through which they became conscious of themselves as a people in relationship to God. And according to the tradition, the last in this series of momentous original events was God's commandment to build a tabernacle, a place where the Presence of God might "dwell among them."

Words of origin are words of power. They speak to our identity as much as to ancient Israel's. As the Passover wording tells us, every Jew in every generation is responsible to know the deliverance from Egypt as a contemporary event, to know that he or she has shared in that deliverance as a son or daughter of the covenant. Christians who take these words of spiritual origin seriously know too that these events of deliverance, covenant, and Presence are living and contemporary.

Let us look at the details of this account to see its significance both in the light of the ancient tradition of Israel and in the light of our willingness to let the images speak to us with power. The first point in the account is simply the command of the Lord that an offering be taken. Moses was to ask for offerings from the people of Israel to make a sanctuary in which their Lord might dwell. If this is indeed God's living word, it commands us also and with power. That Presence is also with us as vividly as with our fathers and our mothers in every element of the biblical account as we hear the Lord's word commanding us to prepare our awareness of that holy center, the tabernacle, that place of dwelling of our Lord with us.

The tabernacle concerns us here, not the temple. Israel's tradition includes at least two symbols for the place of God's dwelling on earth. The temple in the holy city, Jerusalem, is the eternal, ever-present dwelling on the mountain to which we journey, singing our songs of pilgrimage as we approach its gates from east or west or north or south. In the book of Revelation, the city New Jerusalem is itself the dwelling place of God. The numbers of this city suggest its permanence, its spatial dimensions; it is a city built foursquare, with twelve gates facing equally the four corners of the earth.

The tabernacle has a different connotation. It is the tent in which God sojourns, the statement of God present with us in our time, in our journeying through deserts and migrations and changes of state. Its numbers are process numbers: threes or fives, numbers that seem to encourage the mind to move on and continue the series. Its touch with the Divine is an awareness of our identity in God's eyes, where we are in our history. In 2 Samuel 7:5–7, Nathan said to David when he had in mind the building of the temple,

> . . . Thus says the LORD: Are you the one to build me a house to live in? I have not lived in a house since the day I brought up the people of Israel from Egypt to this day, but I have been moving about in a tent and a tabernacle. Wherever I have moved about among all the people of Israel, did I ever speak a word with any of the tribal leaders of Israel, whom I

commanded to shepherd my people Israel, saying, "Why have you not built me a house of cedar?"

The temple is here distinguished from the tent in which God moves with the people.

After the temple was destroyed and the people were in exile, both connotations—the return to that one place on earth and the trust in God's dwelling with the people anywhere—took on special significance. In the book of Revelation in the New Testament, the temple is the image for the new heaven and new earth. In the gospels John uses the tabernacle word for dwelling in a tent when he says of the incarnation: "the Word became flesh and *lived* among us" (John 1:14). The Jewish tradition keeps this tabernacle meaning in its word for the Presence: the *Shekinah*, or literally, the *living* in a tent.

The tabernacle is here, of course, not just one literal tent filled with the Lord's life. It is hard to conceive of God's taking satisfaction in dwelling in a tent or in a house or in any inanimate, unconscious form. The tabernacle is, however, a powerful symbol of God's dwelling among people. For the Christian, its deepest meaning is the Divine Humanity itself, Jesus' life on earth, as John's wording indicates. In a more general sense, it speaks of the receiving of the Divine by the human soul, making conscious, living minds in which God can delight and dwell. In this sense, every human being is called to be a church or holy place, that is, a tabernacle of God, a means for the divine influence to come into the world.

If we are each called to be a church or holy place, what do we need to do then, to bring it to reality? Material for the temple came from afar, from Lebanon, or even "out of heaven from God" in Revelation 21:10. The materials for the building of the tabernacle in Exodus, however, came from the people themselves: good things of quite definite kinds which the Lord had given them. These they brought together according to the divine pattern to receive the Lord's blessing. Every one of the materials Israel was to bring was already within them ready to offer to the Lord's ordering to find its meaning. A tabernacle, or a church, in which the Lord delights is not an unorganized throng of people or of feelings and thoughts within one person. Nor is it a band organized in a selfish way for selfish purposes. It is people who bring together their affections, experiences, knowledge, and powers to be used, to receive and bring forth the Lord's life for good and for blessing. Constrained offerings of merely external, formal profession of religion contribute nothing here either. They are not receptive of the Lord's spirit of blessing. The offerings are genuine offerings, elements lifted up by "all whose hearts prompt them" from love for the Lord and for the neighbor, and the order they receive from the Lord is their own genuine order, set free to function in harmony.

All the wealth of that list of materials is already there, in our inner person. The list itself is a catalog of wonder: gold, silver, and bronze, blue and purple and scarlet stuff and fine twined linen, goats' hair, tanned rams' skins, goatskins, acacia wood, oil and spices, onyx stones, and stones for setting. Each image has its power. First come the precious metals: gold and silver and bronze. The rocks of the earth symbolize permanent, basic truths, such as that life is from God and not our own creation, or that all men die. Metals are mined from rock, but can be molded into many shapes. They are basic truths, which depend for their shape upon circumstances, and are called laws. The gold needed for the tabernacle is awareness of the law of life from God, that is, of good or love itself. The silver is awareness of the laws of usefulness to the neighbor, that is, of truth or wisdom, the form love takes in action. And the bronze, the copper made tough with tin, is the functional, natural good of a life of love and truth in the external world. The tabernacle is not built on arbitrary guesswork. It rests first on knowledge of these functional laws. The first step has to do with love, then, as the base for truth, as our living it makes love complete in action.

Blue and purple and crimson stuff come next. The Lord as the center of love and light is the reality our sun symbolizes. The varied reception of this divine love and light is spiritual color; the absence of it is darkness. Blue is like the dark of night lighted up with white, the color of wisdom and of heaven, of the lighting up of intelligence in the darkness of the mind. Blue-purple, the color mentioned here, is the kindling of intelligence from love to the Lord or the heavenly love of truth. Crimson is red lightened with white or yellow. It represents the fire, or good of love, or the

Lord's love brought out from its presence in the inner person into a more distinctly understood love for the influence of the Lord in human beings. The Hebrew speaks here of "double" scarlet, or mutual love, vividly apprehended. Purple is red and blue together. This purple, of the ancient dyes, was a red-purple, representing the warmth of love for the Lord, or the heavenly love of good. This beauty of color, the delight of the kindling of intelligence concerning things of God, is an essential element in this dwelling place of God with us. It is the law of love received with joy as we begin to be conscious of God's will to be at home in us.

The colors are followed by the white of fine twined linen. Its associations are with truth of celestial origin and with the clean "righteous deeds of the saints" in which their lives are clothed (Rev. 19:8). Readiness to be cleansed and to be clean is part of preparation for God's dwelling. The colors of the cloth and the pure whiteness of the linen are set off by the black of goats' hair, that typical stuff of the bedouin black tents, signaling people on the move or camped briefly for a season. The black wool is the practical external good of mutual helpfulness in learning from the Lord, or in this case, of tent protection for the traveler on the way of life.

The tanning of the rams' skins is literally in Hebrew "reddening" and recalls the red leather tent in which ancient Near Eastern desert tribes carried their sacred objects with them as they journeyed. A *bas relief* of such a small tent set on the back of a camel is carved in stone at the entrance of the ancient temple of Bel at Palmyra in the Syrian desert, and still shows traces of red paint on the stone. Together with these coverings of skins, the tough, fine-grained acacia wood for the frame is a realistically practical element, a strength of functional knowledge of the Lord as sustainer and protector in the immediate, down-to-earth stages of living. The sense of sacred reality within is important, but the wooden frame, the tough-minded courage to see and to deal with practical daily issues without letting go of the sacred, is an equally essential strength for any actual tent or move.

Light for our seeing in the tabernacle is from olive oil in the lamp, that is, the light of the genuine, unselfish goodness of the Lord's own mercy and healing power, not the light of selfish pride or enmity. And to bring the pure goodness with which the Lord blesses the dwelling place to distinct and pleasant consciousness, there are the perceptions of spices for the anointing oil, and prayers and songs of penitence and praise going up as spiritual incense. Finally, there are the onyx and other precious stones for the ephod and breastpiece. These are specific and clearly defined doctrines concerning the Lord's kingdom, shining with the changing light of every varying shade of truth and love as new vision brings new insight.

This is a long list of specific meanings. It seems somehow too good to be true. Were nomads of that early time aware of all of this when they used their sacred tent? Doesn't the list read more like a kind of late and arbitrary game imposed by Worcester or

Swedenborg? Is this just another scheme designed to give a sense of power to those who know the answers?

I think not. All ancient peoples seem to have had a sense of powers in the world around them. A living tree, the earth, a rock, a mountain, a flame of fire, each had its own distinctive power not to be taken lightly. I think of a recent sunset. Its power for me was not the series of colors and shapes. The same colors reproduced on film or by a play of lights on fountains are striking, but they do not break in on me with another dimension and make me listen. Ancient peoples knew meaning breaking in. They would not have used Swedenborg's eighteenth-century Western words to convey the meanings. We might not either. But his words are witness to the reality of that other side of experience. He brings to the conscious, verbal side of me a wealth of emotional reality. And I regain, in my inner world, at least a little of the wonder of real meaning in the nature of things, of which I had been deprived.

The implication of God's command to make the offering for the tabernacle is that all these materials, all the essentials for the building of that holy center where God would live within the human heart, were already there in the possession of the people. They needed only to be brought to light, by being willingly offered to the Lord, to come to conscious power and meaning in a coherent whole. It is as if the typical black tent of some ordinary human journey were found to be furnished with treasure within, to be a habitation fit for the adventure of encounter with the Lord and King. It is like receiving a glorious, unexpected present.

If we let this section of Exodus speak to us as Word of God, we become aware of a wealth of varied gifts and experiences already within our inner person, ready to be brought to light. We have looked at the material in this catalog of wonder: the gold, silver, and bronze, the blue and purple and crimson yarns and fine white linen, the black goats' hair, red-tanned rams' skins, goatskins, acacia wood, oil and spices, onyx stones, and stones for setting. We have begun to speak of the symbolism of these materials. They have to do with love as the reason for truth, with awareness that love and truth must be actually received and lived in order to be understood. They have to do with the stirring of beauty and excitement when the mind is lighted up with new insight, with the joy of cleanness, the fear and joy together of being ready for a move, the wonder of lighting a light, the pleasure of sudden awareness that smells good or shines like a gem, the flare of color in a desert place.

We have begun to speak of these symbolisms. And yet we know intuitively that there is no single, final meaning in any of these images. It is frightening in a sense to realize there is no one interpretation or authority to fall back on, to tell me the final meaning they should have for me or what my inner life is like. And yet, it is partly because of this that they are such powerful symbols of the realities of the inner life. They are not fixed. They are the essential materials for the sanctuary in which the Lord would live with me in my life journey. I must take the responsibility for letting them speak to me, to know the power of what my bronze or blue or pure white linen means for me. But if I hear these words, I can no longer avoid the knowledge that these things are there within. I sense their power to help me know the Presence of the living God, the kingdom of God in the midst of me.

What, then, does all this have to do with me in my life here and now?

I think for me, it is the gift of knowing who I am. It is the potential of looking to my origins and knowing the presence of my Creator dwelling with me. These offerings are not strange to me. I have a sense of the power of love and truth, of the color and fragrance and light added to life by new awareness, of the need and joy of cleansing, of the fact that I do move and grow, and of ways leading to unknown parts just now beginning to open before me in the journey of my growing. The promise of this account in Exodus is not that these are suddenly handed to me. We all have moments of insight like this. As isolated moments, they often seem to give a momentary life and then be gone. The promise here is that these aspects of my being belong together, giving a spiritual harmony to my experience. In these my Maker wills to live with me and be my strength, my Lord. I have a wealth within. I am alive not only to the outer world around me, but to the deeper levels of my life. I am prepared to go on the adventure of my life, to find the God who made me, and to become myself.

· *Meditation* ·

Sit quietly and prayerfully for a moment. Recall the beginnings of the people of Israel, God's call to Moses, the exodus from Egypt, the covenant with God at Sinai that created a people conscious of its relationship with the Lord of history. Feel their sense of God's presence and God's power in history. Now keep this quiet and prayerful openness of mind, and ask God's blessing and protection on the openness, and recall the beginnings of your spiritual history, the moments that spoke to you of your relationship with the meaning of your history. Feel your sense of God's presence and God's power that have brought you to this moment.

And now read again the Lord's Word to Moses in Exodus 25:1–9, and hear it as spoken for you by the God who created you:

> The LORD said to Moses: Tell the Israelites to take for me an offering; from all whose hearts prompt them to give you shall receive the offering for me. This is the offering that you shall receive from them: gold, silver, and bronze, blue, purple, and crimson yarns and fine linen, goats' hair, tanned rams' skins, fine leather, acacia wood, oil for the lamps, spices for the anointing oil and for the fragrant incense, onyx stones and gems to be set in the ephod and for the breastpiece. And have them make me a sanctuary, so that I may dwell

among them. In accordance with all that I show you concerning the pattern of the tabernacle and of all its furniture, so you shall make it.

Lord, thank you that you made me and gave me
life and love.
Thank you that you will to dwell with me.
Help me with my fear of finding so
much within.
There is so much I hardly know, and yet somehow
I know that I am on a journey in my life, though
its beginning and its ending are both beyond me.
Help me with my fear of things too big
for me.
But thank you for that sense of meaning and of
journey. I could not live without them.
Thank you for the gift of hunger for your presence
in my life.
Thank you that I can trust myself to you and
know that you go with me.
Thank you, Lord.
Amen.

2

They shall make an ark of acacia wood; it shall be two and a half cubits long, a cubit and a half wide, and a cubit and a half high. You shall overlay it with pure gold, inside and outside you shall overlay it, and you shall make a molding of gold upon it all around. You shall cast four rings of gold for it and put them on its four feet, two rings on the one side of it, and two rings on the other side. You shall make poles of acacia wood, and overlay them with gold. And you shall put the poles into the rings on the sides of the ark, by which to carry the ark. The poles shall remain in the rings of the ark; they shall not be taken from it. You shall put into the ark the covenant that I shall give you.

Then you shall make a mercy seat of pure gold; two cubits and a half shall be its length, and a cubit and a half its width. You shall make two cherubim of gold; you shall make them of hammered work, at the two ends of the mercy seat. Make one cherub at the one end, and one cherub at the other; of one piece with the mercy seat you shall make the cherubim at its two ends. The cherubim shall spread out their wings above, overshadowing the mercy seat with their wings. They shall face one to another; the faces of the cherubim shall be turned toward the mercy seat. You shall put the mercy seat on the top of the ark; and in the ark you shall put the covenant that I shall give you. There I will meet with you, and from above the mercy seat, from between the two cherubim that are on the ark of the covenant, I will deliver to you all my commands for the Israelites.

The inmost thing in Israel's tabernacle was the ark, the point of actual meeting with God's Word. And the inmost of a live church, or mind, is the part which hears the Word of God as commandment, applied to life, as the living thought of God. And so, as the first section of Exodus 25 on the tabernacle described the materials needed that the Lord might "dwell among them," this second section on the ark concludes, "There I will meet with you, and . . . I will deliver to you all my commands for the Israelites."

The tabernacle is a "tent of meeting," where we meet the Living God. "I will meet with you, to speak to you there. I will meet with the Israelites there, and it shall be sanctified by my glory. I will consecrate the tent of the meeting and the altar" (Ex. 29:42–44). The effective center of the meeting described here was the ark with its testimony within, that is, the Word or Truth of God in its power.

This is the tent of meeting, the meeting of the divine transcendent Other and the human mind. For some, this meeting means an experience of ecstasy, a heavenly escape from the bounds of the finite and of this world. For Israel, it meant the mystery of the divine Word that called the children of Israel to live the life of God's pure Will in the world, accepting the limits of the human mind and will. The image for that transcendent Otherness is the pair of cherubim. The image for the Presence of God's Word here in this world is the chest of wood, the ark, with God's commandments within. And the image for the mystery that brings these two together is the gold or love.

The first to be mentioned is the ark, the specific symbol of God's Presence. In later times, the ark dwelled invisible behind the veil of the Holy of Holies. But early records show the ark going ahead of the people on the march "to seek out a resting place for them" (Num. 10:33). It was when the priests bearing the ark entered the Jordan that the waters parted for the people to pass through (Josh. 3:15). It was the ark that devastated the Philistines (1 Sam. 5). And it was when Uzzah, unauthorized and unprepared, put his hand on the ark that he died, and David feared to bring it into Jerusalem (2 Sam. 6). In Israel's tradition, the power within it was God's Presence in the Ten Commandments, the most important testimony to God's Word.

It is when we hear the Lord's commandments in order to do them that the power of the Lord to save and bless becomes real. John's statement of this is the same truth that was represented by the manifest Divine Presence in the ark of the testimony: "They who have my commandments and keep them are those who love me . . . and I will love them and reveal myself to them" (John 14:21). The ark commands the attention not of the natural level of a person, which could almost be identified, so to speak, as a sort of immortal animal, but of the inmost, spiritual level which knows the Lord and draws support and guidance consciously or unconsciously from God.

The ark, like the frame of the tabernacle, was of acacia wood. This desert hardwood was not a fruit tree valued for the food it gave, but valued for its own sake. It is the type of mind that is strong in resolve, from the knowledge that the Lord has conquered evil. The dimensions of the ark, related to the numbers five and three, symbolize this knowledge of the divine protection in all the length and breadth and depth of human life.

The next element mentioned is the gold, the essence of goodness, or love itself, the connection between the human and the Divine. The wood was to be overlaid with gold, both "from the house side," as the Hebrew says, and from the outside. The ark was gold, then, as well as wood. The commandments were to be seen neither as arbitrary human rules nor as ways for us to set up an account to gain reward. Commandments are not always verbal rules at all. The symbolic power of an action or of a concrete example speaks aloud in the history of Israel, in God's act to free Israel from Egypt, in the life of Jesus, or in the parables of the Bible. The commandments are the living of

God's will, the enjoyment of the Presence of the Lord, letting the Lord's love and mercy be the center and power of life.

The rings and staves were the same combination of wood and gold, of human and divine. They were to carry that Word of God wherever the people went, into all circumstances and states of life. The rings themselves are the joining of good with truth. The definite command that the poles never be removed from the rings underlines the constant readiness for application to life.

The cover of the ark was of pure gold. This is the "mercy seat," the word for covering over sin or guilt. It is the word *forgive* in Psalm 79: 8–9

> Do not remember against us the iniquities
> of our ancestors;
> Let your compassion come speedily
> to meet us,
> For we are brought very low.
> Help us, O God of our salvation,
> for the glory of your name;
> deliver us, and forgive our sins,
> for your name's sake.

This is the word *atonement* in Israel's Yom Kippur, or Day of Atonement, one of the most sacred of Israel's yearly solemn festivals or "meetings" with God. It is this mercy, this divine forgiveness, this awareness of God's pure goodness with no evil at all, not remembering past sins against us, which overlies the Word of God's commandments as we take them home to our hearts.

Finally, the two cherubim were of pure gold alone. Cherubim in the ancient Near East were great, winged guardian figures, part human, part animal, appearing in carvings on the thrones of kings or at the entrances of palaces or temples. Ezekiel 1:5–14 gives a detailed description. In the prophet's vision, the cherubim were

> four living creatures . . . they were of human form. Each had four faces, and each of them had four wings. Their legs were straight, and the soles of their feet were like the sole of a calf's foot; and they sparkled like burnished bronze. Under their wings on their four sides they had human hands. . . . [T]heir wings touched one another; each of them moved straight ahead, without turning as they moved. . . . [T]he four had the face of a human being, the face of a lion on the right side, the face of an ox on the left side, and the face of an eagle. . . . In the middle of the living creatures there was something that looked like burning coals of fire. . . . The living creatures darted to and fro, like a flash of lightning.

Others of these creatures had the body of an ox or lion or bull. The cherubim in Solomon's temple were said to be ten cubits (or about fifteen feet) high (1 Kings 6:23). In one description of the ark, the Lord is seen as "enthroned on the cherubim" (1 Samuel 4:4). In the symbolism of Psalm 18:10, they are associated with the wind, as God

> rode on a cherub and flew;
> he came swiftly upon the wings of the wind.

Ezekiel saw the cherubim in his vision of God enthroned in the temple. The seraphim of Isaiah's vision of God are probably also these numinous guardian beings (Isa. 6). In Revelation 4–6, they are around the throne of God in heaven.

Ezekiel, Isaiah, and Revelation all suggest the mysterious nature of these living creatures, seen indeed, but seen only in vision at the boundary of human sight and where God's Presence or heaven begins. In Genesis 3: 23–24, after the man and woman had made their choice to eat of the tree of the knowledge of good and evil, the LORD GOD sent them "forth from the garden of Eden . . . and at the east of the garden of Eden he placed the cherubim, and a sword flaming and turning to guard the way to the tree of life." The choice to go the way of human reason, persuasion, and rationalization is followed by the protection of the way of return to Eden, lest the tree of life be profaned and humankind destroy itself. The cherubim are mysterious and totally good protecting beings, guardians of the transcendent.

The cherubim are "of one piece with the mercy seat." They spread their wings "above, overshadowing the mercy seat with their wings" of mercy and protection, of support, and of power to rise to the heights. Their faces, turned one to the other and to the mercy seat itself, speak of love to the neighbor and to God, the Divine Goodness from which they spring.

The innermost part of the human mind, that edge of conscious awareness and unconscious creative power, of earthly beings and the Divine, is imaged in the ark with the cover of mercy and the cherubim above. Here we meet the Lord. The Lord commands us to prepare the tent of meeting and the ark in order to meet with us. The innermost mind is not the whole of human awareness. All life depends on God, and the Divine is received in many different ways in different states of being, both consciously and unaware. Yet, that the Divine Presence may be received at all and life on earth continue, there must be somewhere the awareness of that Presence here described.

It is a familiar religious truth that the Presence of the Lord and the awareness of heavenly reality are not rewards of human intelligence or study. They are gifts given in a setting of trust and mutual love. It is true again that, for adults, innocent trust and love do not feel entirely natural, but come from the Lord's goodness. Divine goodness, received consciously, is Divine mercy. Such trust and love are the cherubim: "There I will meet with you, and from above the mercy seat, from between the two cherubim that are on the ark of the covenant, I will deliver to you all my commands for the Israelites."

The offerings for the tabernacle symbolized the wealth already there within the deep levels of the human mind. The ark of the testimony symbolizes the contact with the Other. This account in Exodus speaks to us of the transcendent power of each reality imaged in the symbols, the gold, the blue, the linen and black wool, and all the materials within, the ark and cherubim, as present now as at any time of ancient origin.

· *Meditation* ·

Sit quietly a moment and ask the Lord to be with you as you quiet your mind and prepare to turn to the Word of God.

Read again Exodus 25:10–22 with your mind open to hear it as God's Word to you:

> They shall make an ark of acacia wood; it shall be two and a half cubits long, a cubit and a half wide, and a cubit and a half high. You shall overlay it with pure gold, inside and outside you shall overlay it, and you shall make a molding of gold upon it all around. You shall cast four rings of gold for it and put them on its four feet, two rings on the one side of it, and two rings on the other side. You shall make poles of acacia wood, and overlay them with gold. And you shall put the poles into the rings on the sides of the ark, by which to carry the ark. The poles shall remain in the rings of the ark; they shall not be taken from it. You shall put into the ark the covenant that I shall give you.

Then you shall make a mercy seat of pure gold; two cubits and a half shall be its length, and a cubit and a half its width. You shall make two cherubim of gold; you shall make them of hammered work, at the two ends of the mercy seat. Make one cherub at the one end, and one cherub at the other; of one piece with the mercy seat you shall make the cherubim at its two ends. The cherubim shall spread out their wings above, overshadowing the mercy seat with their wings. They shall face one to another; the faces of the cherubim shall be turned toward the mercy seat. You shall put the mercy seat on the top of the ark; and in the ark you shall put the covenant that I shall give you. There I will meet with you, and from above the mercy seat, from between the two cherubim that are on the ark of the covenant, I will deliver to you all my commands for the Israelites.

Let your mind turn to one commandment you hear the Lord speaking to you—Thou shalt love the lord with all thy heart—Thou shalt love thy neighbor as thyself—Honor thy father and thy mother—whatever one it is that comes to you. And now, in your mind, take the tough strength of fine grained acacia wood and make an ark to put the commandment in, a functional, strong wooden chest, with rings, always ready to take that commandment with you as you go in life, to take in intact, that nothing weaken it or destroy its sacredness. Feel the power of that commandment as you let it go with you as you visualize yourself doing what you do in your home, at work, and in the street.

Now take pure gold, of pure love, and cover the strength of the ark of that commandment with mercy, turning your mind to the Lord's goodness going with you, to the Lord's love as the strength of your keeping that commandment, giving the commandment the power of love to be accomplished, and see the Lord's mercy go with you with its power in your home, at work, and in the street.

And now take the pure gold of that cover of mercy and visualize its shining strength form a beautiful, living, winged, protective figure on each end of the cover of mercy, on the edge, the limit, where your ark ends and heaven begins, and see the power of the hosts of heaven go with you as you move in the strength of that commandment in your home, at work, and in the street.

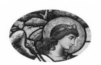

Lord, thank you that your mysterious Presence is
revealed not to the subtleties of intellect, but to
each one who turns in simplicity of heart to know
your will, to do it.
Thank you, Lord.
Amen.

3

The LORD spoke to Moses, saying: Command
the people of Israel to bring you pure oil of
beaten olives for the lamp, that a light may be
kept burning regularly. Aaron shall set it up in
the tent of meeting, outside the curtain of the
covenant, to burn from evening to morning
before the LORD regularly; it shall be a statute
forever throughout your generations. He
shall set up the lamps on the lampstand of pure
gold before the LORD regularly.

*A*ccording to the rabbis, Israel saw a depth in God's
goodness to them in the fact that God not only
created and loved them but also told them through the
scriptures about that creation and that love, so they
would know it consciously. So the tabernacle and the
ark within it symbolize the dwelling place where the
Divine is not only present but where the divine
Presence is known. The light that sheds this knowledge is the subject here.

People can look on the same thing in very different lights. A child may see in grass and flowers their

pleasantness to touch with his bare feet and smell with his nose. A farmer may see them as food for cattle, a botanist as instances of species differentiation. An adult absorbed in other interests may not see them at all. A war may look in one light brilliant and glorious, in another horrible and wrong in its cost in human suffering, in another painful but necessary as a step toward justice. The prophets and the Psalms ask us this question: In what light does God see our history and our world? What would it be like to see in the light of goodness and truth itself, the light of the Lord's own mercy and power to heal? What would it be like to make love the basis for wisdom?

The light for the tabernacle was from oil of olive, pure and beaten. The oil is the symbol for love, associated with joy, with the touch of healing, and with the anointing of a priest or king. It symbolizes heavenly divine good. The word *Messiah* means literally "anointed with oil." The two olive trees on either side of the lampstand in Zechariah's vision are the two Messiahs, or literally in Hebrew, "the sons of the olive" (Zech. 4:14). The Messiah is love giving light to the world, and John speaks often of that light as he sees Jesus as Messiah: "I am the light of the world. Whoever follows me will never walk in darkness but will have the light of life" (John 8:12).

When the people brought the oil, Aaron was to set the lamps in order outside the veil of the testimony in the tent of meeting. People are needed to beat swords into ploughshares or to beat olives in a press or mortar into pure, fine oil. People who have done the beating see their ploughshare or their oil with respect; and the people were to bring their beaten oil and make the lampstand of pure gold, as they had the cover, the cherubim, and the fittings for the ark. The stand held seven lamps of gold, and these were to be kept filled and burning from evening to morning every night, making light continually.

The people have a necessary part here. But the references to Aaron and to the curtain between the ark of the testimony and the lamps show that we are dealing with more than the ordinary conscious level of the people's experience. Aaron is the priest. As Moses symbolizes a truth that cannot be heard or perceived directly, Aaron is the teaching of good and truth in a form that people can hear. The priest, the spokesman and teacher, represents the Lord's love of saving, the part in us that mediates, explains, and loves to save, that draws us to the Lord.

Aaron is the one to keep the lamps in order. There is a proper order used elsewhere for laying a table for a meal (Isa. 21:5), drawing up troops in strategy for battle (Judges 20:22; I Sam. 17:8), or setting an argument in order for a legal case (Job 13:18). Aaron is the priest in us, and not the trickster, the debater, or the seeker after personal reputation; Aaron is the one there to mediate, to order the strategy of our understanding as we begin to bring our holy things to consciousness.

The lamps were outside the veil of testimony. Inside was only the ark with the Word itself, that inmost Presence of the Lord where the power is known at a level too deep for words or conscious apprehending. The part of the tent of meeting outside the veil is the interpretation of the Presence in relation to the motives and the choices of human life. It is here that the light comes, within the specific context of living what is good or true in the limits of an existing situation. The innermost truth is always too much, too powerful, to be contained within our limits. But unless the attempt is made to see its interpretation within the limits, it does not come to light and life at all. So we are asked to bring our oil that love may be the light in which we see the things of God, but we are also asked to respect the veil between the lighted and the innermost ways of knowing. On this boundary of conscious and unconscious we need our Aaron as spokesman for our Moses.

Psychologists since the eighteenth century have made us all aware of the power of the unconscious. Jung saw the Ego and the consciousness as a small segment of the person, as compared to the personal and then to the collective unconscious. The Ego with its conscious analysis of itself and others, its carefully preserved image of itself that it shows to the world in interactions with people, and even its areas of personal unconscious, the feelings and the unseen motivations relating to its personal world, is still not the larger segment of the person. The anima or animus that the man or woman can come to know as inner partner, that other side with which he or she functions as a whole person, and the collective unconscious make up by far the larger segment. In this larger segment of the person Jung found the Self, the deep identity, the center of our real decisions, of which the conscious, Ego choices are the afterthoughts.

Jung saw religious sacraments and symbols as appropriate means for dealing with these unconscious powers. He encouraged his patients to find and use their individual religion in coming to their awareness of their deep Self and in finding a sense of meaning in their existence. He criticized traditional religion, however, for its rigidity and its failure to let the power of symbol live and reach maturity in individual Selves.

We have been following Swedenborg's approach to the Bible in this treatment of the tabernacle. Swedenborgians, like members of any religious group, succumb, of course, in many ways to the temptation of rigidity in religion. But Swedenborgians have a strong respect for the power of symbol. For Swedenborgians, the collective unconscious is the world of spiritual reality through which divine love and wisdom reach humankind and without which we would die. For Swedenborgians, the power of symbol is the power that creates the universe, now as in the past, as each person seeks to realize that Self that is in the process of creation, learns to be a functional form of love, and sees in the amazing reality of the human being the pattern of the universe. For Swedenborgians, too, the Self is in the larger segment, not in the area of the conscious Ego. The Self gains strength from its membership in the spiritual world, as it finds more and more its own distinct identity and its relationship with the Divine. And for Swedenborgians, these biblical narratives of the tabernacle and the ark can bring awareness of that membership. The narratives are living Word of God, not only in their literal history, but as each person comes to meet the symbols in that history, and lets the symbols come alive. And the literal history itself is a symbol of the spiritual journey of every man and every woman.

The light of the tabernacle is the symbol of our bringing to consciousness the inner, deeper meaning of God's Word for us. In our lives, we encounter lights of many shades and colors. This light of the tent of meeting is what we have felt of the Lord's own love, the Good itself. We bring the oil, for all our love is from the Lord, really ours because it is a gift, really given. We bring the oil for the lamps to bring to light for us the reality of that dwelling place of God with us, including the reality of the veil. And if in some way we get used to seeing in that light, to any degree at all, we find increasing strength in awareness that the depths within us are potentially powers for good. For all the creative momentum of the universe supports our finding of our deep distinct identity in the world of which God is ultimately the light.

What would it be like to see, and then to walk, in the light of the Lord's mercy and healing power?

· *Meditation* ·

Sit quietly a moment. Visualize the lamps before the veil that hides the ark. Feel the difference of that inner, timeless world behind the lamps and veil, from the outer world of physical things and confusion in time.

Now open your inner eyes and ears again as you read again Leviticus 24:1-4, and let its symbols be a way for God to speak to you.

> The LORD spoke to Moses, saying: Command the people of Israel to bring you pure oil of beaten olives for the lamp, that a light may be kept burning regularly. Aaron shall set it up in the tent of meeting, outside the curtain of the covenant, to burn from evening to morning before the LORD regularly; it shall be a statute forever throughout your generations. He shall set up the lamps on the lampstand of pure gold before the LORD regularly.

Visualize the clear, golden olive oil, pure oil of love of joy, of healing, of anointing priests and kings, giving its light in that part of life that you can see, that part separated only by a veil from the reality of Love itself in all its power. Rest for a moment in the joy of being in the light of Love. Feel the warmth and the power of that light pouring down upon you, surrounding you with good.

And now turn your mind to some decision you have to make or some person with whom you have a relationship, and see that decision or that person in the light of Love itself. Feel the warmth and the power of that light pouring down upon that decision or that person, surrounding it or him or her with good. And now let go, and let the power of the Love work, and see your decision or your person in that light, and be thankful.

Lord, thank you that your Love is so close to us,
your Love so amazing, so real I cannot imagine,
much less see it,
there every moment, in all the power that makes
the universe,
coming in goodness unto me.
Thank you, Lord.
Amen.

4

· THE ALTAR OF SACRIFICE ·

EXODUS 20:24–25

You need make for me only an altar of earth
and sacrifice on it your burnt offerings and
your offerings of well-being, your sheep and
your oxen; in every place where I cause my
name to be remembered I will come to you
and bless you. But if you make for me an altar
of stone, do not build it of hewn stones; for if
you use a chisel upon it you profane it.

We have seen three essential elements in Israel's
tabernacle: the offerings of the materials for it to
be built at all, the making of the ark to receive the
Word of God, and the lighting of the lights to let the
whole be seen. These things are real. But they are cer-
tainly not the whole of anyone's inner life. They are
the good side. And as I think of them, and think of letting them come into my inner life with power, I find
another side of me that also needs to be heard.

The wealth of materials for a tabernacle, the ark of
the Word of God, and the light of Love itself from the
Presence of God? Those don't feel like what's in me.

The things I notice are the strangest combinations of fears and hurts and unusual, embarrassing memories, some joys and hopes, some wants and worries, some plans, and some plain, blind panic. I do sometimes have a sense of peacefulness or beauty or awe that I am alive at all, and, yes, sometimes when I need it, a strength that gives me courage. But usually I feel the strange things, and I have the feeling that, if I open the door to them, all sorts of horrible, worse things will come. Even if that holy center is there, how in the world can I get what's in my mind to come near it? And is it safe?

And so I know that, if the dwelling place of God is to be real for me, the journey toward it won't always be easy. It feels frightening and painful to deal with those dark things, even though I tell myself the pain is a pain of growth. But no significant journey is easy. And I know it is my journey. The choice to begin it and the timing of it are mine. And so I am ready to go on and ask the Lord how to come near the Presence of God within in ways that lead to healing and not to hurt.

The first step in coming near is building an altar of sacrifice. And instantly my mind brings up its objections. Now, wait a minute. Killing animals on altars doesn't sound like a very promising start. Those verses in Exodus are grim. What possible use can those instructions be to me? Haven't we learned beyond all doubt that God asks no such thing? We know the Lord desires "steadfast love and not sacrifice, the knowledge of God rather than burnt offerings" (Hos. 6:6). "To do justice, and to love kindness, and to walk humbly with your God" (Micah 6:8) has always meant more than "thousands of rams, with ten thousands of rivers of oil" (Micah 6:6). Obviously, such sacrifices have never been what God really wanted of people, and they aren't now. God does not desire death and pain, and God has not changed.

These questions are valid and cannot be left without response. A first step is to consider the meaning of sacrifice for ancient Israel. For us today, the word *sacrifice* has almost entirely negative connotations: "to offer to God, to give up, destroy, permit injury or forego a valued thing for the sake of something of greater value, to sell at less than the supposed value," according to Random House. The root meaning of the word, however, was its meaning for Israel. They meant quite literally to "make holy" (*sacer* and *facere*), to bring to God, usually with great joy.

Some sacrifices were wholly given to God as burnt offerings that went up in flames. The far more common thing to do with sacrifices, however, was to eat them. This was the rule with the peace offerings. Ancient Israel lived mainly on the milk and cheese of sheep and goats, and then, later on, of larger cattle, as they settled and began to raise crops. To kill one of those animals for food was for a rare occasion only, a special guest meal or celebration, a yearly family gathering (1 Sam. 20:6), a fulfillment of a vow or giving of thanks (Ps. 116:17f), or a coronation (1 Sam. 11:15). When Israel went to Gilgal to crown Saul king, "they sacrificed offerings of well-being before the LORD, and there Saul and all the Israelites rejoiced greatly"

(1 Sam. 11:15). Another time, Samuel, the seer, went to a high place to "bless the sacrifice," to which some thirty people had been invited, and persuaded Saul to stay and eat a special portion of the meat as an extra guest (1 Sam. 9:13–24). A key word at these festival meals is rejoice, and Israel's celebration of any public worship was in Hebrew called typically rejoicing before the Lord their God (Dt. 16:11).

All eating of meat involves sacrifice, the giving of one life that another may live. Some religions have responded to this with abstinence from meat, and others with the reminder that all eating of any food is to be done reverently as worship. Israel's response accepted the distinctiveness of eating meat and asked a special reverence at any accepting of another breathing "soul of life" (Gen. 1:24) for food. This response symbolized, at least in part, sharing in a common life with all creatures who have breath, realizing that we continue in life only through receiving it from others.

Israel's kosher meat observance is a literal reminder of this attitude to life. The life of an animal is its blood as well as its breath. And so, according to the tradition, when after the flood humankind took the step that separated them from their original membership in the family of moving, breathing creatures when all lived peacefully on green plants, the one part of the animal not to be eaten, was the blood. Blood and breath were too holy, too closely connected with the original gift of life, and the blood was to be poured out to God, the giver of life. So God blessed Noah, and said

Every moving thing that lives shall be food for
you; and just as I gave you the green plants, I
give you everything. Only, you shall not eat
flesh with its life, that is, its blood. For your
own lifeblood I will surely require a reckon-
ing: from every animal, I will require it and
from human beings. . . . .

Whoever sheds the blood of a human,
    By a human shall that person's blood
        be shed;
For in his own image
    God made humankind.   Gen. 9:3–6

In Israel's sacred eating of meat, then, the blood was
sprinkled on the altar, the fat and kidneys burned upon
it, the breast and right thigh especially handled, the
thigh given to the priest, and the remainder returned
to the man who offered it as a feast for him and his
friends. In this slaughtering of the animal, there was
the relinquishing of one's own proprietorship, the
acknowledgment that all life is a gift. The feast became
a feast from the Lord, which otherwise might have
been mere enjoyment of one's own good things. To eat
our life food in this manner is to hallow the actions of
our lives, not to do them from habit or necessity or as
our own empty pleasure, but "rejoicing before the
Lord," living new life freely in what we do. The Lord's
word about sacrifice in this passage in Exodus does not
ask an arbitrary work of supererogation in coming to
the Holy Place. It asks that we bring the substance

of our actual lives to the Lord, to be touched and to be hallowed.

Samuel went to a "high place" to consecrate the sacrifice. An altar is typically raised up, a spiritual high place, as opposed to a depression. It might be raised of earth or of stones. Good earth receives seeds and brings forth fruit. It is our longing for goodness that we raise before the Lord, the certainty that all goodness has its source in the Lord and the desire to do that goodness. Once there, it remains a height in the mind, a place of sureness and perspective as we go down from it to work or return to it for direction.

Stones, on the other hand, are firm truths that do not shift around. Some people work more naturally from good or feeling and receiving, and others from truth or searching and understanding. There is no value judgment here. Some can build an altar of stones more easily than one of earth. The only provision for the stones is that we accept each stone in its wholeness and not hew it to our own devices. The essential for the altar is not that it be earth or stones, but that it be real and of our building. To demand immediate demonstration of feeling from those who need to work first in thought is inconsiderate and frightening. To demand words from those who need to live first with feeling states or intuitive awareness is hopeless and frustrating. Worship, like love, is comfortable in an atmosphere of appreciation for what each person offers freely and with integrity; it is uncomfortable with demands laid on arbitrarily from outer space. Either altar is good. Either needs only to be raised in the heart whose altar it is.

The animals to be offered are our affections, our feelings for what we desire as good. Animals have a strange power to engage our feelings. Visualize for a moment a cat, a lion, a snake, a lamb. Each brings out a different and quite distinct response, a quality in us that needed only the symbol to come alive. That spark of identification with the cat's distinctive kind of playfulness, combined as it is with a readiness to pounce, is that little leap or tug inside us in response. So all animals symbolize feelings, some wild, some tame, all powerful, but not in a language we understand in words.

The animals Israel brought regularly to the altar were from their flocks (sheep, lambs, goats, or kids)—that is, innocence and love in the inner person—or the bigger work animals of their herds (oxen, bullocks, and calves)—that is, feelings for good and truth in the external person in action in the world. These feelings are the power behind all our inner states, all our relationships, and all our actions. New life here, renewing love from God, is mercy and knowledge of the Lord, in which the Lord does indeed come near and bless the life brought near for hallowing. According to Swedenborg, that is what blessing is: "that which has within it *being* from the Divine" (*Secrets of Heaven* §8939). All we have said about Israel's use of the altar of sacrifice has to do with awareness of that which is of God in all of life.

While this is very beautiful, we have not yet responded to one of our original questions. It is, after all, a "slaughter altar." How does the pain of death fit with what we have been saying? This question is real. The animal we eat does die, and Israel had not yet hidden that fact under the plastic wrappers of the supermarket. To know that what sustains my life is a gift, not mine until I release it and receive it again, to give up my proprietorship, is to experience a dying. True, the flame on the altar is the Love of God in all its light and heat and life. But that flame asks all of me if I am to let it touch my life. To receive my life again in freedom, I must first have given it up. I cannot even approach that Love without being deeply and even desperately conscious of the evil in my own heart. For me as an adult, the innocence with which the Lord unites is the innocence of repentance, of turning back to the Lord as the source of my life.

Death is part of sacrifice. For the Christian, the sacrifices of Israel prefigure that one most significant death, Jesus'. But if we respect Israel's use of sacrifice, it is not in the negative sense of an arbitrary loss, a negative bargain struck with God or a penalty paid for a fault. Rather it is in the sense of a life in which the Love of God comes to us where we are, gives itself to us, touches us, hallows us, and makes us come alive if we give ourselves up to it.

Giving is not without its consequences. There is no coming to the light of that flame that does not show up vividly the strange and the unexpected, as well as the deeply satisfying elements in my inner life. Israel made offerings for sin, defilement, and trespass, as well as for thanksgiving, and knew that these too were part of them and had their place in worship. We will be dealing with them later and with the issue of pain and death. The first step is to know that there is the Holy Place within, that God's Presence is with us to touch the depths of our feelings and of our awareness. But, clearly, this Place will not be functional for us until we bring the feelings to the altar, the actual underlying feelings, whatever they are, that make us do the things we do. But, again, in the very awareness of the strangeness of what we have to bring, the light of the Presence is already working; and the power, the living energy of that light is Love.

· *Meditation* ·

Think back for a moment on the wonder of a holy place within you where God dwells with you, *really* with you. Not with the front you take to church or lay out for the public. But with you, with those fears, hurts, memories, joys, hopes, worries, plans, panics, strengths, and sometimes awe.

Turn to God's Word, and read the meditation Psalm 139:1–4; 13–16:

> O LORD, you have searched me and known me.
> You know when I sit down and when I rise up;
>   You discern my thoughts from far away.
> You search out my path and my lying down,
>   And are acquainted with all my ways.
> Even before a word is on my tongue,
>   O LORD, you know it completely.

· · · · · · · ·

For it was you who formed my inward parts;
>You knit me together in my mother's womb.
I praise you, for I am fearfully and wonderfully
made.
>Wonderful are your works;
That I know very well.;
>My frame was not hidden from you,
when I was being made in secret,
>intricately woven in the depths of the earth.
Your eyes beheld my unformed substance.
In your book were written
>all the days that were formed for me,
>when none of them as yet existed.
How weighty to me are your thoughts, O God!
>How vast is the sum of them!
I try to count them—they are more than the sand;
>I come to the end—I am still with you.

Before that thought had reached the conscious verbal state of being on your tongue, God knew it altogether. Before any inner part of you had come to birth at all, God knew it. And knowing all of what you are, God gave you life and brought you to birth and into being. What is the strangest thought or fear that might come in that strange country of your mind? God knows it altogether and still is there.

Now read again Exodus 20:24–25, and hear God's Word addressed to you to come, to build your altar, to bring your feelings as they are, to receive your life from God, and to be blessed.

You need make for me only an altar of earth and sacrifice on it your burnt offerings and your offerings of well-being, your sheep and your oxen; in every place where I cause my name to be remembered I will come to you and bless you. But if you make for me an altar of stone, do not build it of hewn stones; for if you use a chisel upon it you profane it.

*Lord, thank you that you know me better than
I know myself,
and still you ask me to raise my thoughts or
feelings to be an altar for you
to come to give me blessing.
Thank you that the sacrifice you want is not some
punishment for guilt,
or game of saying the right words, or
proving worthiness,
or bargaining for the right favor for some
move ahead,
but simply coming, as I am, to you who know me,
to let your love touch me and to receive
the gift of life.
Thank you, Lord.
Amen.*

5

When anyone presents a grain offering to the
Lord, the offering shall be of choice flour; the
worshiper shall pour oil on it, and put frankincense on it, and bring it to Aaron's sons the
priests. After taking from it a handful of the
choice flour and oil, with all its frankincense,
the priest shall turn this token portion into
smoke on the altar, an offering by fire of pleasing odor to the LORD. And what is left of the
grain offering shall be for Aaron and his sons,
a most holy part of the offerings by fire to the
LORD. . . . You shall not omit from your grain
offerings the salt of the covenant with your
God; with all your offerings you shall offer salt.

The altar of sacrifice was a way of bringing deep,
underlying feelings, painful as well as joyful, to the
Presence. These feelings were aroused usually by
some special occasion of personal, family, or national
life. There was something of crisis in this slaughter
altar, standing as it did in the courtyard, outside the

holy place itself, bearing the fire that made present Love itself. The lampstand of pure gold with its lighted lamps, within the holy place, but still, of course, outside the veil, also had a sense of otherness about it. It pointed beyond what human eyes can see to Truth itself. Both of these furnishings were awesome witnesses to the Presence in its dwelling place within. The awe is real. But the holy place had also another, more homey and more comfortable symbol of coming into God's presence: the table for the loaves of bread.

The table again was of pure gold in witness to God's love, but the loaves, baked regularly of fine flour grown and ground by people, were the peaceful satisfactions of daily receiving love and strength from God in the normal affairs of life and especially in daily work.

Eating food is perhaps the most basic symbol of needing to be nourished, to be sustained in life. The prophet Joel sees food as parallel to "joy and gladness" in the "house of our God" (Joel 1:16). The mother who nurses and comforts her child and the Lord who says to his disciple, "Feed my sheep" are two vivid images of God's caring love in the Bible (Isa. 66:12; John 21:7). To give and share food is the simplest, most natural act of human caring, and at the same time the most directly open to the Divine. It was the way of sharing in the most solemn act of communion in the ancient Near East, as well as the way of fulfilling the most basic human obligation: hospitality to the stranger. According to the earliest tradition, when Moses and Aaron, Nadab and Abihu, and seventy of the elders of Israel saw the God of Israel at that most

solemn time of the making of the covenant, "they
beheld God, and they ate and drank" (Ex. 24:11).
Again, when the Lord came to speak with him at
Mamre, Abraham's first words to his angel visitors
were an embodiment of the right ethical response to
guests—offering food:

> When he saw them, he ran from the tent
> entrance to meet them, and bowed down to
> the ground. He said, "My lord, if I find favor
> with you, do not pass by your servant. Let a lit-
> ter water be brought, and wash your feet, and
> rest yourselves under the tree. Let me bring a
> little bread, that you may refresh yourselves,
> and after that you may pass on—since you
> have come to your servant."   Genesis 18:2–5

When the angels stayed, the "little bread" became,
of course, a meal of meat and curds and milk, as well as
cakes of fine meal. This is partly normal Near-Eastern
hyperbole, as any ancient or modern Israeli, Arab, or
Greek might speak of what he would set before a guest.
But bread is the common, staple food, the symbol for
all food in general, for all that nurtures and satisfies,
including the celestial food of God's love for humankind and human love to the neighbor. According to
Swedenborg, bread is love brought to its simplest,
most basic form, on earth and with each person, as well
as in heaven (*Secrets of Heaven* §2177). The table for
the loaves of bread means bringing normal, human

daily work to the Lord's Presence to find peaceful satisfaction in it.

What agrees with our life is food for us and satisfies. Some satisfactions are more intense than others, however. To gain immediate satisfaction only, no matter what the consequences to others, brings fear of retaliation. To hold on to inflated or temporary satisfaction brings fear of loss. So Aaron, the priest in us, who desires our peace, puts our loaves in order each week for the Sabbath, as he does our lamps each day.

The greater part of daily work is not made up of spontaneous acts of affection. Work requires thoughtful effort. It requires planning for what will happen, allowing for contingencies, evaluating methods. The mentality that serves work best is used to taking responsibility, depending on its own resources, judging success or failure in terms of outside standards, putting personal needs aside, our own and sometimes those of others, in order to get the job done. Tensions over performance, or over meeting others's standards, are so common that they almost seem to be part of having a job. This mentality may seem perhaps most apt to set us on our own, apart from God. The powerful emotions—anger, fear, or love—touch us enough to drive us to our depths, to meet our Lord. This work mentality seems just to separate. But if persons can find no peace or sense of meaning in the work that takes the major part of their days and greatly influences their feelings about themselves, then something is missing in their tabernacle. It is good to be reminded that, when we get pulled off base by regular or by unusual demands on our time, one element even now functioning in our inner self is the priest within, who has the desire, the energy, and the skill to order our priorities so that we may find peaceful satisfaction.

Israel's tabernacle provided ways to deal with both the regular and the occasional demands of work. For the regular, the loaves were set in order every week on the table in the holy place. For the occasional, special bread offerings were brought to the altar in the court-yard as needed. For both, the bread was to be of fine flour. Work takes many forms. It may be public serv-ice or highly public leadership at the executive level, flying airplanes or repairing their engines, writing books or washing floors. For some, it may be dealing with not having a job. For some, it may be work never acknowledged, the hard work of planning, marketing, cooking, cleaning, driving, washing, teaching, but taken for granted because it is expected of a mother or a father. What makes it "fine" is not its public image or prestige, but its motivation and its actual use to persons in society.

Each kind of work involves some kind of value, or it would not be done at all. It may provide a living, foster an enormous ego, be the facade for rebellion against a parent, or be a sensitive way of serving God and coming alive by using one's best talents to contribute creatively to the common good. Negative or hidden motivations can create problems. But the work mentality itself can also split our calculating self from our essential feelings, and splitting thought from feeling is destructive. Neither accumulation of accomplishments without feeling nor spontaneously fluctuating expression of every feeling without thought for consequences makes fine flour. Work done intelligently and from a spirit full of the Lord, wise thought for others and for oneself, put into action, is the flour for these loaves of bread.

To the flour, oil was added. If fine flour is needed for this bread, it is no wonder that pure olive oil, symbolizing God's mercy, is needed too. All life and wisdom and love are, of course, from God, as well as all good food and grain. But specific knowledge of God's mercy to all is essential to the sense of the Lord's presence for our good.

To fine flour and oil is added the frankincense of intelligent gratitude. It is hard to think of a more pleasant fragrance than that of freshly baked bread, but the fragrances of spices for anointing oil and for incense were also part of the atmosphere of the tabernacle and of worship. Odors have to do especially with perception, and the pleasant odors of incense with grateful, joyful perception of truth. The underlying nature of a person corresponds closely to the atmosphere in which he or she can breathe easily and to what odors he or she finds pleasant. Pure frankincense is inmost truth, clarified from the falsity of evil, and perceived with joy. Frankincense was a part of the special combination of spices used to make the cloud of incense always before the ark in the tent of meeting, a special combination sacred to that purpose, and never to be used by human beings themselves (Ex. 30:34–38). Frankincense alone was used by human beings, however, and was associated with the luxury of King Solomon (Song of Songs 3:6), the fragrance of the beloved, the bride-to-be (Song of Songs 4:14), or, together with gold, as a symbol of the wealth of all the world of nations brought in praise of God to Jerusalem (Isa. 60:6). The odor of frankincense mingled with that of fresh bread was indeed joyful perception of God's goodness in all. And that is worship.

The bread was also to have salt. The salt of the covenant of God (see Num. 18:19 and 2 Chr. 13:5) is the desire that love has for wisdom in order to do good wisely and the desire that wisdom has for good in order to live and to be fruitful. This element makes heavenly food savory and assimilates it to life. To be without it is to know truth and have no care for living it, to have no savor.

The bread of regular, daily work was to be twelve loaves of generous size, after the number of all the tribes of Israel and of the fruits of the tree of life, to represent all the varieties of joy and satisfaction of working with the Lord, conscious of the Lord's presence and purpose. The twelve loaves were in two piles of six, six being the number of work days and representing the full state of labor. The two piles of six, side by side, symbolized the Lord's blessing given equally to those who sought to do what was true or right and to those who sought to do what was good. This was the "show bread," the bread of the Presence, placed by the priest on the table within the holy place for each Sabbath. The word for "show" or "Presence" here is literally "faces," that is, before the face of God, in the presence of all that is from the divine Love, such as innocence, peace, joy, or heaven itself with those who receive it (*Secrets of Heaven* §§9545–9546).

Loaves could also be brought to the altar to be offered for special needs connected with daily work. The break of occasional, varied kinds of work might be cakes baked outside the oven and simply anointed with oil (lesser, external duties, subordinate to our chief work) or hastily cooked on a griddle or boiled in a pot like dumplings (incidental duties of all kinds) or even flour ready for the baking (a duty not yet seen clearly enough to take a particular shape) (Lev. 2). All work involves some satisfaction. If it is simply dropped and left to go stale, it can be moldy or dry drudgery, involved in all kinds of negative bargaining. If it is brought to the table or the altar, its satisfaction is recognized, and the bread is transformed by the spirit of God who gives it life.

The loaves of the Presence on the table in the holy place and the bread brought to the altar for offering were eaten with joy. In both cases, a "memorial," a part that brought the Presence of God to active memory, was not eaten but burnt, sent up to God to symbolize the Divine actually present. For the bread of the Presence, this memorial was the frankincense; for the bread of the offering, it was "a handful of the choice flour and oil" and "all its frankincense," the "handful" meaning that the person making the offering was to take hold, or love, with all his or her strength or soul. The rest was for Aaron and his sons, to be eaten, "a most holy part of the offerings by fire to the LORD."

This part, which the priest in us eats, means the sense we have of working as of ourselves as we carry our goals into life, knowing that the power to work is from God and is God's power with us.

The offering of my bread is this combination of my taking hold with all my strength, giving my effort to my work, and at the same time trusting the accomplishment and the outcome of each action to the Lord, because the Lord's strength is present. When I bring to the Lord my thought for daily use, which I hope to live in my work, penetrated with the oil of God's mercy to me and to my neighbor, and I catch the scent of the joy of God's gifts, a quickening fire kindles and unites with them all and brings new life. This is the Lord's life brought to life in the work of persons in this world.

The priest was to eat this bread in a holy place since it was a holy of holies of offerings. When Jesus himself drew near and went with the two disciples on their way to Emmaus, they did not recognize him, for the crucifixion had put an end to their hope that "he was the one to redeem Israel." But "when he was at table with them, he took the bread and blessed, and broke it, and gave it to them." And as the bread was broken to be eaten, in the simplest human act, most open to the Lord, it became again the bread of life and Presence, and they knew that it was he.

· *Meditation* ·

Turn your mind back to one typical working day, the effort you put in, the work accomplished, the times of joy or satisfaction. Be open to your feelings. What kind of satisfaction did you have? Do you feel tense or peaceful as you think of it? Did only one part of you find satisfaction or was the whole of you content? Where did you find the satisfaction? In achievement? In the simple things of life like having enough to eat or seeing a sunset or seeing someone smile? What are you aware of in yourself as you think of bringing your daily work and life to God?

Read again Leviticus 2:1–3 and 13, and be open to the images in it.

> When anyone presents a grain offering to the Lord, the offering shall be of choice flour; the worshiper shall pour oil on it, and put frankincense on it, and bring it to Aaron's sons the priests. After taking from it a handful of the choice flour and oil, with all its frankincense, the priest shall turn this token portion into smoke on the altar, an offering by fire of pleasing odor to the LORD. And what is left of the grain offering shall be for Aaron and his sons, a most holy part of the offerings by fire to the LORD. . . . You shall not omit from your grain offerings the salt of the covenant with your God; with all your offerings you shall offer salt.

What element speaks to you? The fine flour of balanced thought and feeling? The oil of mercy? The incense of God's goodness in all things? The salt that makes satisfaction good and part of ordinary life? The very fact of bringing your satisfaction to the altar and not letting it go stale?

Now think back to your own working day, and ask the Lord to help you bring it as an offering, and receive a holy, peaceful satisfaction as the Lord gives you the blessing of wholeness and new life.

Lord, thank you that you are with me in the simplest, daily parts of life.
For my life is full of so many little things,
and if I could not find you there, I would be lost
and lack direction in so much.
Thank you that the simplest act of giving and
receiving food is most open to your Presence.
Lord, help me with my priorities.
Help me to take hold with my full effort, and then
trust all results to you.
And thank you that I can bring my work to you
and know the taste and scent
of peaceful satisfaction.
Thank you, Lord.
Amen.

6

Now this is what you shall offer on the altar: two lambs a year old regularly each day. One lamb you shall offer in the morning, and the other lamb you shall offer in the evening; and with the first lamb one-tenth of a measure of choice flour mixed with one-fourth of a hin of beaten oil, and one-fourth of a hin of wine for drink offering. And the other lamb you shall offer in the evening, and shall offer with it a grain offering and its drink offering, as in the morning, for a pleasing odor, an offering by fire to the LORD.

If we look at Israel's ceremonies merely as part of history, they may seem like the actions of a very external people, performed with a gross, if not altogether mistaken, idea of the God they worshiped and with an equally obscure idea of worship. Seen in this way, the solemn slaughter and burning of two lambs a day seem simply the remains of the ancient history of a barbarous age.

But what, then, is the element of vitality that has preserved such a detailed record of these sacrifices to the present day? Why are ceremonies like these found mingled with the high ethical teachings, psalms, and prophecies that have been the foundation of the most sensitive social ethics, high religion, and hope for so many generations? And why is it that these ceremonies, related in such minute detail, seem so plainly to be commanded by God as essential for Israel? It seems impossible today, at least, to take them as essential to a relationship with God.

The approach we have been taking sees the Bible as, indeed, a revelation from God, partly clear and partly obscure, as people have been able to receive it. It sees the symbols in the Bible as speaking throughout, with power, of the most central elements in the religious life, whether to ancient or to modern men and women. And these morning and evening sacrifices of the lambs, offered for Israel day by day, deal now, as they have always in the past, with the ups and downs and changes, the timing of the inner life.

The working day outdoors in Israel's climate is dominated by two twilights: the half light before the heat of the sun strikes the land with fire and energy, an almost savage challenge to getting work accomplished in the face of penetrating power, and the half light of evening, the cool of the day, when breath can again be drawn freely, and a little space of rest and peace is given before the deep blue of the night is wholly present. Evenings and mornings here speak more vividly than in the temperate zones of beginnings and ends, of new life and completion, of creation.

Each morning and each evening has its own sacrifice of a lamb, fine flour and oil, and wine. We have seen that animals symbolize feelings and that meat and bread offerings are to be either burnt or eaten. Animals burnt wholly on the altar are our awareness that good affections are wholly from God and that these affections or feelings can be the means of our knowing our unity, our communion, with God. Animals burnt outside the camp as sin offerings symbolize thorough removal from the heart of feelings and patterns that are destructive. And animals eaten in feasts before the Lord symbolize the nourishing of the mind by God and bringing God's life to practical use in this world. These three elements together picture three essential aspects of the fullness of worship: (1) removing evil, (2) receiving goodness and truth from God, and (3) living in a way that brings that innermost presence of goodness and truth to concrete reality and action.

The morning and evening sacrifices ask for "two lambs a year old regularly each day." The lamb is, of course, a symbol of gentleness and innocence, affectionate and playful, with no apparent desire to hurt and no means of attack. It follows its mother and then its shepherd. It loves play, it loves food and drink, but it will leave everything at its shepherd's call. This yearling lamb is a symbol of positive, active innocence, not a symbol of mere new-born lack of desire to do wrong. The poetry of Isaiah sees the lamb together with the kid, the calf, the cow, and the little child, living in peace with their opposites: the wolf, the leopard, the lion, and the poisonous snake, in that final time of peace itself when the Spirit of the Lord shall reign and the earth be "full of the knowledge of the LORD as the waters cover the sea" (Isa. 11:6–9).

To bring the lamb to the altar and to commit it wholly to the flame are to come to the Lord with positive, lively innocence, knowing it to be the Lord's gift and seeing in it the sacred fire of divine Love. This is to love the Lord "with all your heart, and with all your soul, and with all your might" (Deut. 6:5). This is to trust, and to come near to, the Divine.

We have mentioned other elements in the worship of sacrifice besides this inmost one, namely, purification from destructive patterns and bringing the Presence to use in the world. We cannot always think directly of the Lord. We come down from states of elevation or out from the experience of the innermost to do the work of life and set our minds to attend directly to what needs doing. But at the beginning of the work, while it is still in contemplation, we can, in full view of it, come interiorly to the Lord with the offering of a lamb. And when the work is done, we can return to the Lord with a lamb, acknowledging that what is good is from God. And if this is done day by day—that is, in every state of our lives—good from the Lord can fill our work with living love. Then we will not defile it by trying to make it bolster up dead patterns of our own that struggle so desperately to manipulate and work against the underlying current of life. Life is full of beginnings and endings, and if these be sanctified by the Lord, the whole of life receives a holy power.

Beginnings and endings are different, however, and our coming to the Presence is a different coming from one perspective or the other. Mornings are the inner person, open to his or her real center within, and evenings the external person, coming back from the struggle, the successes, and the pains. Both need to be hallowed in God's Presence.

Mornings are easier than evenings. Before beginning the work or assuming the responsibility, there is a newness, a hopefulness combined with uncertainty, a fear that has a positive potential. The vision of all we hope for is still clean; the dangers, the unpredictable elements, are threatening, often in proportion to the power of that vision.

In the experience of going to a workshop, for example, either to lead it or to take part, there is always some anxiety involved, and it is easy to turn to the Lord for help. The decision to give a dinner or a party may begin with purely pleasant feelings of anticipation, but once the invitations are accepted and all must be organized and ready for that actual moment, tension is present. But having gone to the workshop or given the party and having had the success or the peak experience, the need for help is less clear. We may know our duty, to acknowledge thankfully that the Lord has blessed us and that the kingdom, the power, and the glory are God's. But it was *our* success, after all, and we enjoyed it. There were flaws, granted. It did not come off with all the glory of our dream. But we did it, we made it through, and we deserve to feel good about ourselves.

That second lamb of innocence and innermost centering after the successful event sometimes seems harder to find. The success has become *my* success. And if I set out to lead another workshop or give another party, I now have the negative fear that it may not be as good as the last one, that I may not have as great a success again, and I want to guarantee it by trying the same methods another time. Or if I shared the peak experience, it is now over; I have a similar negative fear of loss of a possession. And where, in this obscurity of evening, is that second lamb?

The key to the problem is in the word *possession*. The second lamb is sacrificed "in the evening," between the two evenings. We have mentioned the two twilights in each day, two times of half light and obscurity. Between the evenings is between the evening and the morning dusk, normally soon after sunset (Deut. 16:6), but in any case before the light of dawn. The two evenings emphasize the light to come, the fact that all obscurities of night are part of the daily change of light and dark that make dawn possible.

The fear of loss keeps saying, "Protect the possession. Don't let it change. Go back to recapture what you had." But nothing, of course, could be more futile or more frustrating. What "between the evenings" suggests is the opposite, the awareness that all beginnings, accomplishments, and endings are part of a living process, that endings are an inevitable part of leading to what is new, and that the process is good. In Hebrew and in Judaism, evening begins the new day. Darkness was there upon the face of the abyss when

God said, "Let there be light." Evenings precede mornings in the poetry of the six days of creation. The awareness of God's creation at work in every evening at the beginning of each new day is an awareness that suggests that second lamb of thanks to God for life itself, the ground of all our work, our intention, and our feeling good.

No living thing can exist for long without real change. Morning and evening awareness of God, day by day, is the bringing of our changes of state to the Lord, seeing the Lord's presence in the changes. It is a relief to read in Swedenborg's treatment of this commandment that angels as well as people in this world are expected to have real ups and downs and changes of state in their growth process. I imagine they are more aware than we are here of a stability underlying the change. But creation is a continuing and a trustworthy life process for us here too. If every morning and evening, every beginning, end, and new beginning, is brought to the altar to be given wholly to the Lord, the whole of life is sanctified and can be trusted, whatever the immediate success or failure.

With the lamb was offered flour and oil and wine. These three—the grain, the wine, and the oil—are the good gifts of the earth as described by the prophets, as well as by poets who lived in the land of Canaan long before Israel (Hos. 2:2; Joel 1:10). Grain is the fruit coming from the goodness of the earth, the truth of good that gives the good distinctive, existing form. Pure olive oil is good experienced as mercy, which soothes, heals, destroys friction, lends taste and consistency to food, or burns with a bright, warm flame: it is a goodness that comforts and heals the spirit.

Fine flour and oil together, then, represent loving thought put into action, permeated and hallowed by a perception of the Lord's goodness to all. They were part of all bread offerings. For morning and evening, the third element, the wine, is added, poured out upon the altar. Wine is water drawn up from the earth by the vine; and as the leaves of the vine sport in the air and sunlight, the water is filled with sweetness and spirit and presented to us in the beauty of clusters of grapes. Water, from its cleansing and life-giving powers, is truth in active, actual form which distinguishes between worthless and good and teaches what is right. The vine may be any human mind that loves to learn such truth, to see it in relation to the Lord's love and life, and to present it to others full of sweetness and spirit. For Christians, Jesus, "the true vine," so lived the truth that he presented it to us filled with his own life. The elements of communion, then—the bread of grain and oil, and the wine—are to be with us, joined with the innocence of the lamb, in every beginning and ending of our life. It is not just a symbolic lamb alone. The wholeness of a meal is symbolized, of eating the food of life, but at these moments offered wholly to the Lord.

The bread for this offering on the altar, like the bread of Presence on the table, was to contain no leaven and no honey. Leaven is the beginning of fermentation or corruption, the thought of self that can make a good action inflated and insincere, and honey a merely natural pleasure unconnected to its spiritual base. Leaven and honey are both good. We are called to be leaven as well as salt, to raise as well as to give savor to the lump. The land "flowing with milk and honey" is our promised land of Canaan with its abundance of delight. When we do what we need to do, in the time between the beginnings and the ends, there must be thought of self. Natural elation and all kinds of natural highs and sensual pleasure are good gifts to be enjoyed, not disdained. There are times when it is right to feel good about ourselves and to focus on that feeling. The question is not whether this is good or bad, but whether it is the right time. Wine, of course, is fermented. Truth is processed, but the love of this sacrifice is a spontaneous gift. Devotion to the Lord that does not lead out there to the world of the senses, where lives are lived and actions are done and enjoyed, is incomplete. But actions done out there without a live connection with that innermost space that can give all, totally, to God, are nothing.

We are asked to be aware of timing, of those moments of morning and evening, of beginning and ending. We are asked at these times to turn to that most sacred innermost and offer it totally, with no thought of self, to the fire. And as we do this, the fire of God's love gives life, and an "odor of rest" or pleasantness, a perception of peace, is the sign of God's communion with us, and hallows all the rest.

· Meditation ·

Relive in your mind, visualizing and letting the feelings be involved, one piece of work you did or one thing you decided to go to.

Relive the beginning. What are your hopes? What brought you to that moment when you knew you would do that action or go to it? What feelings are you experiencing now about this?

Relive the actual experience. What happened? What was successful? What was painful? What feelings are you experiencing now?

Relive the ending. What was it? Was it a success or a failure or a high, a peak experience of yours? Are you afraid of losing it? Is it something you want to go back and recapture another time? Or was it not an ending at all? Was it just a jumble, a loose end dropped somewhere that needs to be picked up and seen before its ending can take place? Do you need right now to find that second lamb and offer it to the Lord and bring your inner work to its completion? What feelings are you experiencing now?

Read again the Lord's Word in Exodus 29:38–41:

> Now this is what you shall offer on the altar: two lambs a year old regularly each day. One lamb you shall offer in the morning, and the other lamb you shall offer in the evening; and with the first lamb one-tenth of a measure of choice flour mixed with one-fourth of a hin of beaten oil, and one-fourth of a hin of wine for

drink offering. And the other lamb you shall offer in the evening, and shall offer with it a grain offering and its drink offering, as in the morning, for a pleasing odor, an offering by fire to the LORD.

Bring to the Lord the beginning you have just relived, and give it, totally, to the Lord, holding nothing back.
Bring to the Lord the ending you have just relived or just experienced, and give it, totally, to the Lord, holding nothing back.

Lord, we get so often lost, and so afraid, and hurt.
Bring us back to you.
Tell us again your love for us, as goodness and as
mercy to us and to all people.
Help us to come to you with the beginnings and
with the endings of our lives.
Help us to see them in your Presence.
Help us to give them, totally, to you.
Bless us, Lord.
Amen.

7

· THE LAW OF BURNT OFFERINGS ·
LEVITICUS 1:1–9

The LORD summoned Moses and spoke to him from the tent of meeting, saying: Speak to the people of Israel and say to them: When any of you bring an offering of livestock to the LORD, you shall bring your offering from the herd or from the flock.

If the offering is a burnt offering from the herd, you shall offer a male without blemish; you shall bring it to the entrance of the tent of meeting, for acceptance in your behalf before the LORD. You shall lay your hand on the head of the burnt offering, and it shall be acceptable in your behalf as atonement for you. The bull shall be slaughtered before the LORD; and Aaron's sons the priests shall offer the blood, dashing the blood against all sides of the altar that is at the entrance of the tent of meeting. The burnt offering shall be flayed and cut up into its parts. The sons of the priest Aaron shall put fire on the altar and arrange wood on the fire. Aaron's sons the priests shall arrange the parts, with the head and the suet, on the wood that is on the fire on the altar; but its entrails and its legs shall be washed with water. Then the priest shall turn the whole into smoke on the altar as a burnt offering, an offering by fire of pleasing odor to the LORD.

The morning and evening sacrifices asked that we be aware of timing, of the beginning and ending points, of the changes in our spiritual lives. The law of burnt offerings, with all its details for what and how, brings us to the issue of specificity. The person bringing the offering is to select a perfect bull, bring it to the altar to the door of the tent of meeting, lay his hand upon its head, slaughter it, skin it, cut it up, and wash its entrails and its legs with water. The same specific directions are repeated in the rest of the chapter for the offering of a sheep or a goat, except that it is to be killed on the north side of the altar, and equally detailed directions are given for the offering of a dove or pigeon. There is no avoiding the specific, graphic details or the direct involvement of the worshipper himself in the details, in this coming to the Lord.

Today we are impatient with such details. We see ourselves as enlightened religious people, and we want to simply "go to the Lord" and feel right with ourselves. We go with our confessions, our fears, our desires to do better, and we hope to receive life and peace. But the spiritual things in us are often obscure, and so our worship is often obscure. We believe that God is with us and that the Lord will hear us and do us good; we humble ourselves in a general way and receive a general sense of protection and benefit. But the respects in which we really, specifically need help are often not distinctly seen; the wrong is not distinctly confessed, nor the good intelligently desired. And so the blessing of the Lord does not come clearly to our perception or come effectively into the particular pattern of our behavior or our feeling that needs healing and new life.

To go to a doctor or to a therapist or counselor with a feeling of discomfort in general is not enough to solve the problem. To confess and to feel bad about sin in general is a destructive religious game that hides the cause and does not cure it. To be willing to face the problem at its source, to be helped to find the original choice, the root of the malfunction, and ask for help— there are the essential steps to physical, psychological, or spiritual health. As Søren Kierkegaard puts it, God's command is never for love in general, or "by the battalion," but in specific, in the particular choice or encounter in which we are actually engaged.

The first choice in coming near to God according to this law of burnt offering is that of the particular offering to bring. To "offer" in Hebrew is to "bring near," and so this choice concerns simply the specific content of what we want to bring near to God, as symbolized by an animal from the herd or flock, a bird, or bread, or other food. For the burnt offering, given totally, as the innermost depth of the person encounters God in his or her aloneness, the underlying feeling was required, as represented by the animal or dove whether other food was given or not. The big cattle of the herd symbolizes patient love of usefulness or service, the lamb or sheep innocent love for God's goodness and mutual love for others, the goat innocent love for the Lord's wisdom and for a life according to it, and the dove innocent love of thinking and communicating truth.

No wild animal is in this list. These are the domestic animals, raised for food to sustain life, all symbolizing patient or innocent love. We are all aware of all kinds of other feelings, and wild animals have both negative and positive symbolism. We will be dealing with wild animals of both kinds before we are through. But they are not for this innermost, total sacrifice. We cannot go to the Lord asking that our loves of excessive food or of superiority to others or of ability to outfox and manipulate others be sanctified and expect an answer of peace. And we cannot complain that we have no innocent love to bring. If we are alive at all, it is because we know sufficient peaceful love to maintain life. We do turn to God when we are aware of the negative side of the wolf or fox in us. But for the strength to meet the wolf or fox, to really meet, enough to realize its positive as well as its negative symbolism for us, we must find and use the source of peaceful power within. We turn to this peaceful love when we approach the altar.

The ox or sheep or goat I bring may be young or old, but for this burnt offering it must be a perfect male. Its male power, the love of the Lord's truth by which the food is multiplied, must be intact. I must find that first choice, that original and begetting source, which brought this feeling into being or that present potency that keeps the feeling strong. I bring this to the altar, to the door of the tent of meeting, that place where the Presence of God speaks within.

Here I lay my hand on it. I accept and feel my full identification with it, not explaining it away, not looking from a distance, but knowing it as a part of me. And now that I have said simply, with no evasions, "Lord, it is I who come," my offering is "accepted" to "make atonement" for me, to lay the cover of mercy over my nakedness as I approach the altar.

And now I kill it. I wholly give it up as mine, holding back no reserve, no string, that it may live from God alone. We all know dreams of dying, that someone else is dying, that I will have to die, that I am trying to put to death someone or something. The reality of moving on from one stage of life to the next often speaks loudly in our dreams, and always, in my experience, with some kind of grief or pain or horror from which I am trying to escape. And yet, we must be willing to move on if we are to be alive at all. To let go and experience the new is not to say the old is vile or wrong or unimportant. We know with our minds that this is true, that moving on to the new is no attack upon the old. But dreams speak from our feelings. And here we know that to let the old die is to feel the pain of loss. We experience the grieving; it is a part of dying to one part of self and rising to new life. I do the killing—I, myself.

But now, suddenly, I am no longer alone. The priest in me, Aaron's sons, who are the Lord's own love of saving, of leading people to love good freely, who draw all people to the Lord in love, "offer the blood." They pour the mysterious power of the life of my offering on the altar and say by their action that all the truth in us, from which love lives and grows, is the Lord's own thought, with strength and depth and breadth to pervade all, and even to let us see some small glimpse of its power, if we will let it.

I, again, must skin the bull and cut it into its pieces, prepare it, as for food. The skin is the most external part, the knowledge of present circumstances and opportunities, which give form to love, but are not themselves a permanent part of the essential being. To make ready for eating, for sustaining life, I must reach the substance of my bull. If the underlying love is reached, the Lord will provide circumstances and opportunities.

And now, the priests put fire upon the altar, fire that is the Love of God uniting with all my feeling and consecrating it as given to the Lord. And they lay wood in order upon the fire and lay the pieces I have cut in order upon the wood that is upon the fire upon the altar. The bull is mine, and I must have known this identification. But as I let go of it and give the Lord's love space to move within me, the priest in me orders it, puts it into the right sequence and proportion, so that I am not left standing beside a mass of stuff too big to handle but can see the meaning of the order of the parts. Now they are ready for the flame.

The intestines and the legs I wash with water. These are the practical functioning parts that receive food and that carry the animal into action. In actual doing, there is always a mixture of motives, of self-interest or self-indulgence or claims of personal possession to justify using others for my ends. These parts need washing, and I must do this before my whole mind can be open to the Lord's Presence.

And then the priest in me burns the whole upon the altar, and my offering is given to the Lord, complete. The law of burnt offerings brings out unmistakably the amazing interaction between the offerer and the priest within me as I approach the Lord. It is "I," my conscious self, who finally realizes I must take that particular offering to the Lord. And a shiver of fear runs through me, and I stand there, shocked, and cowering, and feeling totally alone. And sometimes at that point I panic and decide I am alone, with a job I must handle by myself; and so I run away, and the offering does not take place, but waits for another time. But sometimes at that point, I stay still long enough to breathe. And I recognize, in the realization of the inevitability of that offering, that there is a strength within, a priest already present, drawing me to the Lord. With that knowledge of a strength and love of God already there, I can face the responsibility I alone must take in carrying out the offering.

For the Christian, Jesus is that amazing interaction, that Presence in an existing human life, made manifest as light and life. He is the wood upon the altar, the fire of the sun, that is, embodied in living trees, made visible to people. And that living fire, present in his life as light, is Love.

The Presence of that Love is already within, as we know always at some level, enlightening, strengthening, the Source of life itself. That Love is at the same time the Presence to which we come, taking our responsibility for being specifically who we are. When these come together, the offering is complete.

· *Meditation* ·

Stop a minute. Be quiet and see if there is one thing insistently buzzing around somewhere in your mind, a guilt, a fear, a tension in a relationship, a worry, whatever, that you know is one of those innermost things that will need to come to the altar of God.

Now turn your mind to visualize the Lord with open arms of love. Breathe in and feel the Lord's strength and life flow into you, giving life all through you, filling your heart, overflowing and filling your whole body. Feel the Lord's Love as goodness and mercy pulsing in you, the strength of your life, and the life of every living creature. Rest in that Love. Feel yourself supported by the life of the universe, divine Love.

Now read again Leviticus 1:1–9, hearing the Lord speak to you from the tent of meeting:

> The LORD summoned Moses and spoke to him from the tent of meeting, saying: Speak to the people of Israel and say to them: When any of you bring an offering of livestock to the LORD,

you shall bring your offering from the herd or from the flock.

If the offering is a burnt offering from the herd, you shall offer a male without blemish; you shall bring it to the entrance of the tent of meeting, for acceptance in your behalf before the LORD. You shall lay your hand on the head of the burnt offering, and it shall be acceptable in your behalf as atonement for you. The bull shall be slaughtered before the LORD; and Aaron's sons the priests shall offer the blood, dashing the blood against all sides of the altar that is at the entrance of the tent of meeting. The burnt offering shall be flayed and cut up into its parts. The sons of the priest Aaron shall put fire on the altar and arrange wood on the fire. Aaron's sons the priests shall arrange the parts, with the head and the suet, on the wood that is on the fire on the altar; but its entrails and its legs shall be washed with water. Then the priest shall turn the whole into smoke on the altar as a burnt offering, an offering by fire of pleasing odor to the LORD.

Now bring your offering, the love that bids you bring to the Lord, that real, insistent, innermost thing in you, and offer it there before the Lord, as the words direct.

*Oh Lord, Source of my life, my Creator and
Giver of new life, my Redeemer, my Sustainer,
thank you for your amazing grace.
You cover my nakedness.
Your love is here with me in every moment, and
yet you ask me to come to you.
Thank you Lord.
Amen.*

8

· PEACE OFFERINGS ·

LEVITICUS 3:1–5; 7:11–17, 29–33

If the offering is a sacrifice of well-being, if you offer an animal of the herd, whether male or female, you shall offer one without blemish before the LORD. You shall lay your hand on the head of the offering and slaughter it at the entrance of the tent of meeting; and Aaron's sons the priests shall dash the blood against all sides of the altar. You shall offer from the sacrifice of well-being, as an offering by fire to the LORD, the fat that covers the entrails and all the fat that is around the entrails; the two kidneys with the fat that is on them at the loins, and the appendage of the liver, which he shall remove with the kidneys. Then Aaron's sons shall turn these into smoke on the altar, with the burnt offering that is on the wood on the fire, as an offering by fire of pleasing odor to the LORD.

. . . This is the ritual of the sacrifice of the offering of well-being that one may offer to the LORD. If you offer it for thanksgiving, you shall offer with the thank offering unleavened cakes mixed with oil, unleavened wafers spread with oil, and cakes of choice flour well soaked in oil. With your thanksgiving sacrifice of well-being you shall bring your offering with cakes of leavened bread. From this you shall offer one cake from each offering, as a gift to the LORD; it shall belong to the priest who dashes the blood of the offering of well-being. And the flesh of your thanksgiving sacrifice of well-being shall be eaten on the day it is offered; you shall not leave any of it until morning. But if the sacrifice you offer is a votive offering or a freewill offering, it shall be eaten on the day that you offer your sacrifice, and what is left of it shall be eaten the next day; but what is left of the flesh of the sacrifice shall be burned up on the third day.

... Speak to the people of Israel, saying: Any one of you who would offer to the LORD your sacrifice of well-being must yourself bring to the LORD your offering from your sacrifice of well-being. You own hands shall bring the LORD's offering by fire; you shall bring the fat with the breast, so that the breast may be raised as an elevation offering before the LORD. The priest shall turn the fat into smoke on the altar, but the breast shall belong to Aaron and his sons. And the right thigh from your sacrifices of well-being you shall give to the priest as an offering; the one among the sons of Aaron who offers the blood and fat of

the offering of well-being shall have the right
thigh for a portion.

The law of burnt offerings asked us to look inwards
to meet the Lord in the intensity of our aloneness.
The law of morning and evening sacrifice also asked us
to turn to that innermost sense of the Lord's Presence
at moments of beginnings and endings. In both, our
offering was wholly burnt. Our morning and evening
bread was unleavened, pure of all corruption. The
symbols here are clear: all good is wholly from the
Lord; we turn to God alone.

Peace offerings are different. They are the sacrifice
we eat. We bring leavened as well as unleavened bread
for our feast, and we share our meal with family and
friends. We are asked to see the good in us, in those
around us, and in the things we enjoy. We are asked to
accept joy.

We saw that peace offerings were the most common
form of sacrifice in ancient Israel, so much so that
Israel's word for joining in public worship was the
word *rejoice*. The great seasonal festivals of praise and
thanksgiving, celebrations of victory or harvest or of
living in peace in the land, of return to health, safe
journey, or just waking up alive, all called for joy before
the Lord. To sing, to dance, to make music, to shout,
to clap the hands, to feast together were normal elements in Israel's worship of God. The peace offering
or festival meal enjoyed with others before the Lord
was one of the most obvious symbols of thanking God
for the blessings of life.

Blessings were not reserved for some distant time to come in Israel. The ox or bull from the herd of Leviticus 3 was the symbol of material benefits like health, prosperity, or service in the world. Other animals that could be used were the sheep or goat, the sheep meaning innocent love, as for the Lord or for other people, and the goat enjoyment of wisdom in a spirit of charity toward others. For this offering, the animal could be male or female. The offerer could bring either his awareness of the begetting principle and the receiving of new generating principles from the Lord (symbolized by the male) or the enjoyment of the fruits of the principles of love (symbolized by the female). Israel's psalms of praise, like her command to love, speak not in the abstract or in generalities but give the reason for the praise. The praise or thanks were given for benefits experienced in a particular success or harvest in this world.

The theory that all good is from the Lord is pure and simple. The experience of enjoying the actual victory or harvest is always mixed, however, partly to do with God's pure gift and partly with our conduct, right or wrong, of the event. This back and forth creates a problem with accepting joy. And it is precisely to this back and forth that the commandment for the peace offering speaks.

The first steps are the same as for the burnt offering. The worshipper himself brings his bull or sheep or goat, acknowledges that it is his by laying his hand on its head, and gives it into God's hands by doing the slaughtering himself. The priest then throws the blood against the altar, attributing all life and truth to God. But now the rest is not committed totally to the flame. When we rejoice over a good thing the Lord has given us to do or to receive and when we communicate it to others, we accept it really as ours, expressing it as of ourselves, giving it the unique form that is our life. The greater part of the meat, then, we eat or distribute to those close to us. But as we enjoy and communicate the wisdom and goodness of life, we cannot avoid the knowledge that in the most inner parts the Lord sustains them and gives them their power, and so the inner fat and some of the inner parts of the sacrifice are sent up in smoke to God by the fire on the altar.

In a land as sparse as Israel's, fat had good associations. True, a human heart that became "fat" became insensitive and could not understand (Ps. 119:70, Isa. 6:10). But the fat of animals was the choicest part, and the fat of the land was the richest of its grain and wine and oil (Numbers 18:12–32). The inner fat of the animal had special significance. The priest was to burn the fat that covered the intestines and all the fat that was on them, the two kidneys and the fat that was on them, and the caul or appendage to the liver. The intestines are the parts that absorb nourishment from food, and the fat on them is pure nutriment, deposited for instant use by the body as needed. This fat symbolizes the memory, the wonder of a memory of good things learned from the Lord, providentially stored and ready to come to consciousness in time of need for the nourishment of the spirit.

The kidneys in the Bible, as in other ancient understandings of the person, were seen as the seat of the emotions, a part of the body most sensitive to spiritual atmospheres and critical for health. Their function of separating the pure and impure serum of the blood, returning the pure to use and diverting the other, symbolizes the power of discerning between truth and falsity. The abundant fat about them is the memory of the delight of straight thinking. This function and the memory stored with it are to be put totally into God's hands.

In the Bible, the liver is associated with the temper of mind, the attitude of heart, the weight or dignity or glory of the person. It has a similar separating function of preparing blood for the heart, removing bitter, acrid, and useless particles, and sending on a fluid pure, rich, and sweet, ready for any use. And so it symbolizes the faculty by which bitter, acrid, and useless things are removed from the mind and the thoughts of the heart are made loving and charitable. The delicate fat that it deposits is the joy of loving, charitable thought. A healthy person needs a liver. The problem is not that bitter, acrid, or useless things appear in the mind. The problem is only if there is no power to discriminate and recognize that they are bitter and let them go. The liver, then, is for us to eat and to enjoy, but the fat and the appendage attached to it are given to the flame.

If the offering is a sheep, its fat tail symbolizes the last and lowest things of the kind represented by the head. And as the head of the sheep represents love to the Lord from perception of God's merciful love, the tail represents a grateful memory of the goodness of God's creation and providence. The fat tail is given with the other inner fat totally to God.

All power has its source in God, and sometimes this is what we must experience. Here, however, we experience the interaction between what lies rightly in our power and what does not. All blood, or life itself; the fat, the amazing, gracious memory of good and truth stored deep within us; the kidneys, seat of the emotions, and separator of truth from falsity; the appendage attached to the liver with its ability to discriminate among the intentions of the heart—all these are for God's hands alone. Now, the breast and the right thigh are given a special, mediating place, as the portion of the priest within us, the part of us that mediates and is merciful, drawing us to good and to the Lord. As the intestinal fat surrounds the vital inner organs, so the breast surrounds the heart and is elevated and given to the priests to eat. The right thigh, that strong, muscular part connecting our feelings and our vital organs with our power to move and to stand firm, the good of love, is given to the priest who offers the blood and fat. Our priest part brings to consciousness the life from the Lord that comes through into our ability to love and be of use. And now the remainder of the meat, the greater part of the offering, is for the offerer, the familiar human part of us, the worker and enjoyer in this world.

Bringing to the altar means, of course, being open to the inner Presence of the Lord, and the meal we share symbolizes our sensing the heavenly things the Lord gives us, filling us with love and peace. God's love and truth are given to us and added to our lives to nourish the inner angelic part of us, to make us strong. But if we forget these gifts are from the Lord, thinking that truth has its source in our intelligence, our souls begin to be separated from their life, and spiritually to die. And so it is commanded that we eat neither the fat nor the blood, but enjoy our gift of life from God.

Our feast demands fresh bread as well as meat. We have seen the symbolism of bread and oil, interior satisfaction of useful work, or love expressed in action. A loaf of bread is given to the priest to lift up and eat before the Lord, to show that we receive the satisfactions of life from God, and the rest is eaten with the meal. Both leavened and unleavened breads are eaten. This is the peace offering in which the joy of ordinary good work, with its mixed motives, is brought to the Lord as good. Self-interest too can be real and good. It has its place in this sacrifice in which the actual joy of human beings comes peacefully into the Presence of God and finds its blessing.

Two kinds of peace offerings are described, and these again bring out the rightful interaction between the human and the Divine. The meat of the sacrifice of thanksgiving is eaten on the day of offering it, with none left until the next day. Spiritual joys and loves are not things we can lay up or provide for ourselves. They are living and precious only when continually new from the Lord. A votive offering or vow promised ahead to the Lord or a free will offering recognized as owed to the Lord and so given has more of our own foresight in it and can be eaten on the next day also. Our own prudence is often good, though different from the selfless response of pure, spontaneous thanksgiving. We need to provide ahead and provide for ourselves. But anything kept until the third day is the confirmation of our own prudence, justice, or generosity, making it the source of our religious practice. This is neither eaten nor burned by the sacred flame into ascending smoke. It is to be burnt with the fire of destruction, into the symbol of annihilation: ash.

Symbols seem always to have at least two opposing meanings. So fire destroys, but it also is the touch of love that brings new inner life. The peace offering brings us face to face with two sides of satisfactions in this world. For adults at least, satisfactions seem always to be mixed: partly impure and overly self-seeking, always presenting us with tension between joy in our own strength or sense of what is good and in God's totally self-giving love.

It seems so simple to accept joy. And yet I make it hard. I get caught between the two sides of satisfaction, needing some justification of my own for the joy or some sort of reassurance that it will really be my sort of joy and not break my categories wide open, when I, where I am, think to accept the gift as mine. And as soon as I start questioning whether I deserve the satisfaction, my guilt begins to work: "The joy can't really be for me. It won't last. It can't be real. They are just saying that to make me feel better." Or my fear: "If I let myself like it, I'll lose it, and that will hurt.

Something awful will happen, so it's better if I feel bad now. Then I won't be disappointed." Or my desire to have as owner: "I'll take it. I'll take it as mine and not let go of it. I'll make it last. I'll make it happen again!"

The peace offering is exactly what it says. It brings peace between the inner person, longing to be open to God's goodness, and the outer, so caught in deeds and justifications that it cannot trust the joy. How does it do this? It gives me the way to go peacefully to God with my successes, the things I have done well. And then it shows me the way to give to God the kidneys and the fat. It helps me to know, with humility and with relief, that I am to give the kidneys, that the source of my feelings, of my power to care, is the major element in my discrimination of right from wrong or true from false—not my own wisdom—and that the power to care is a gift from God, not under my control. And it helps me to know, with equal humility and relief, that I am to give the fat, that my deep memory, which is such a threat to me when I try to control it, is not meant for my control. I cannot make the time bombs of memory disappear or tell the uneasy sense of ambush down that path to go away. Thank God, my Lord does not expect me to. But I can put my memory in the Lord's hands and trust the Lord to be with me in what-ever comes, not letting more come than I can handle and reminding me of strengths and goods in past experience when this is what I need. The conscious memory, that glory of being human which so often seems to function as an instrument of hell, can be an amazing instrument of God's grace. The peace offering, the feast of our thanksgiving, of our enjoying our success, puts memory in God's hands.

When we read the accounts of ancient Israel's joy before the Lord, we wonder. Is it all right to take such joy in good things in this world? Is this a joy of simple, primitive people, no longer possible for modern men and women? Is it like seeing the immediate delight of a child in food, in sleep, in life itself, that is so moving partly because it is something we no longer have? When we see ourselves before God, shouldn't we as adults think more of sin and of responsibility than of joy? The Word of God to Israel speaks unmistakably of sin and of responsibility. But it speaks even more unmistakably and emphatically of joy, of gratitude and awe that God works in the whole of Israel's life in the world. Israel knew what we sometimes forget: that the courage, the depth of being that is needed to face sin and responsibility, come only on the grounding of accepting joy in God's goodness. Without the experience of joy, we are only playing games on the surface of our responsibility, not dealing with the real. The prior reality that lets us respond at all is God's goodness. The Bible rests on this assertion: God created us for good. Love's joy is to give itself. God's Love has no manipulation in it. It is wholly for our good. Because Israel's faith was grounded in the Lord of history and of creation, she could bring her offerings for victories or harvests confidently to the Lord and accept her joy in them as gifts from God. She could know joy.

What shall we do with the good things that come to us? What shall we do with joy? Let us enjoy them. Let us go peacefully and eat our offerings in God's presence. And the parts we eat, together with the parts we give totally to God shall be "for a pleasing odor, to the Lord," that is, for our inner peace.

· *Meditation* ·

Sit quietly a moment. Think of one thing you would like to bring peacefully to God: your health, the power to use your mind or body; the power to do your job; the power to love another person; any one good thing you have received or done.

Are other people near you in the good thing you have received or done? Is your thought of them with you as you think to bring your offering to God?

Turn your mind to the Lord, source of all life and power and good, who called you into being, your true Father and true Mother who has more love to give you than you could ask or think. Feel the joy of that love, breathe in its goodness, rest in its strength. See that love coming also on any you know as near you, in this offering to God.

Now read again Leviticus 3:1–5; 7:11–17, 29–33.

> If the offering is a sacrifice of well-being, if you offer an animal of the herd, whether male or female, you shall offer one without blemish before the LORD. You shall lay your hand on the head of the offering and slaughter it at the entrance of the tent of meeting; and Aaron's

sons the priests shall dash the blood against all sides of the altar. You shall offer from the sacrifice of well-being, as an offering by fire to the LORD, the fat that covers the entrails and all the fat that is around the entrails; the two kidneys with the fat that is on them at the loins, and the appendage of the liver, which he shall remove with the kidneys. Then Aaron's sons shall turn these into smoke on the altar, with the burnt offering that is on the wood on the fire, as an offering by fire of pleasing odor to the LORD.

. . . This is the ritual of the sacrifice of the offering of well-being that one may offer to the LORD. If you offer it for thanksgiving, you shall offer with the thank offering unleavened cakes mixed with oil, unleavened wafers spread with oil, and cakes of choice flour well soaked in oil. With your thanksgiving sacrifice of well-being you shall bring your offering with cakes of leavened bread. From this you shall offer one cake from each offering, as a gift to the LORD; it shall belong to the priest who dashes the blood of the offering of well-being. And the flesh of your thanksgiving sacrifice of well-being shall be eaten on the day it is offered; you shall not leave any of it until morning. But if the sacrifice you offer is a votive offering or a freewill offering, it shall be eaten on the day that you offer your sacrifice, and what is left of it shall be eaten the next day; but what is left of the flesh of the sacrifice shall be burned up on the third day.

. . . Speak to the people of Israel, saying: Any one of you who would offer to the LORD your sacrifice of well-being must yourself bring to the LORD your offering from your sacrifice of well-being. You own hands shall bring the LORD's offering by fire; you shall bring the fat with the breast, so that the breast may be raised as an elevation offering before the LORD. The priest shall turn the fat into smoke on the altar, but the breast shall belong to Aaron and his sons. And the right thigh from your sacrifices of well-being you shall give to the priest as an offering; the one among the sons of Aaron who offers the blood and fat of the offering of well-being shall have the right thigh for a portion.

Now bring your good thing to the Lord. And, especially, put the source of your feelings, your motivation, and your memory into God's hands, releasing them to become instruments of grace and goodness in your life.

O Lord, thank you that all the strength of my life,
all my reason for being, is yours already,
that I can trust my whole self to you, even my
successes and my fear of joy,
and those near to me, and know that you are God.
Thank you that you are good, that your mercy
and your loving kindness are forever.
Thank you, Lord.
Amen.

9

The LORD spoke to Moses, saying, Speak to the people of Israel, saying: When anyone sins unintentionally in any of the LORD's commandments about things not to be done, and does any one of them:

If it is the anointed priest who sins, thus bringing guilt on the people, he shall offer for the sin that he has committed a bull of the herd without blemish as a sin offering to the LORD. He shall bring the bull to the entrance of the tent of meeting before the LORD and lay his hand on the head of the bull; the bull shall be slaughtered before the LORD. The anointed priest shall take some of the blood of the bull and bring it into the tent of meeting. The priest shall dip his finger in the blood and sprinkle some of the blood seven times before the LORD in front of the curtain of the sanctuary. The priest shall put some of the blood on the horns of the altar of fragrant incense that is in the tent of meeting before the LORD; and the rest of the blood of the bull he shall pour out at the base of the altar of burnt offering, which is at the entrance of the tent of meeting. He shall remove all the fat from the bull of sin offering: the fat that covers the entrails and all the fat that is around the entrails; the two kidneys with the fat that is on them at the loins; and the appendage of the liver, which he shall remove with the kidneys, just as these are removed from the ox of the sacrifice of well-being. The priest shall turn them into smoke upon the altar of burnt offering. But the skin of the bull and all its flesh, as well as its head, its legs, its entrails, and its dung—all the rest of the bull—he shall carry out to a clean place outside the camp, to the ash heap, and shall burn it on a wood fire; at the ash heap it shall be burned.

No one is sinless. And knowing ourselves as we do, we know we would be foolish to expect our children to have only good impulses or to see the path of wisdom always. Sometimes we guide them wrongly from our lack of understanding or from sympathy with their wishes, for often what we know to be hurtful seems to their excited desires a great thing. They do, of course, do wrong. What we can expect is that, in quiet states, they will talk with us about what they have done or wished to do, to learn what is hurtful and what is not. If they do this, we are content, for they are learning.

As with our children, so with ourselves. No one knows all the varieties and phases of evil to which he or she is liable. We learn our depths of evil and of good by living, and not by thinking about them only. As we grow in awareness of our inner selves and as new circumstances come in our outer world, we will, of course, do wrong. It is as important for us as it is for our children to understand the error and to seek the wisdom to do better, for we are learning. And so the sin offerings speak not to retribution from a God eager to punish, but to understanding the affections of our hearts and the sources of them as we learn to identify what hurts and to avoid it, to find integrity and wholeness.

Errors recognized, excused, and still persisted in do not receive much sympathy. Unintentional errors under pressure of wrong guidance or of unfamiliar feelings are easily forgiven. But these too cause injury and unhappiness and must be dealt with. They can become fixed in our behavior by being continued. But they are forgiven, and the mind is freed from them when they are identified and discontinued.

The sin offerings described in Leviticus 4 are for this sort of unintentional error. Sins done "unwittingly" like this raise the question of how they are recognized as sins. Whose judgment calls them sins? Or who has been at fault in doing them in the first place? Leviticus 4 identifies four sources of unintentional error. The part we have quoted deals with the priest. The chapter goes on to speak of the congregation, the ruler, and, finally, the ordinary citizen. What different mistakes in judgment are distinguished in these four cases, then? And how do they apply to us and to our learning from mistakes?

We have met the priest in us, the part that draws us to the Lord, whose purpose is our good. Can our priest, our conscience, be mistaken? The priest is the idea of God and the influence of God's goodness among people. The sin of the priest is the perversion of this idea and influence, leading us to seek what is not good in the name of the Lord. How does this happen unintentionally? A child will often hold literally and rigidly to one rule he was taught: one way to make "real" scrambled eggs or one way to hold his hands in prayer, and announce instantly the other way is wrong. We smile, but we respect the conscientiousness involved. The danger comes when we do this in God's name, as adults, holding our belief blindly for ourselves and others. In the history of religions, there seems to be no sin that people have not committed conscientiously in the service of their gods. Absolutizing our human judgments, convincing ourselves that conscience or principle demands this or that, and forcing ourselves to go against our intuitive sense of what is loving can cause extreme suffering for ourselves and others. The Crusades and Inquisition were extreme cases, but there are countless others, some hardly noticed because they are so common. Conscientiously picturing the joys of heaven as pleasures of glory, eminence, or indolence, making self-gratification in the future the highest end to be sought (with certain arbitrary conditions), has led directly away from the heavenly joy of closeness to the

Lord in the goodness of a life engaged in loving others. Conscience can sometimes lead to hell on earth.

When conscience is in error, we must retrace our
steps, bringing our hearts to the Lord just as they are,
with their desire to do good and with their unintentional guilt. We must learn from God's Word, not
from our imagination alone (or from our friends or
parents) what God is and wills. We must be ready to
turn away from what we then know to be evil and
painful in the presence of God's goodness. Our priest
is open to the Lord. Our priest is our consciousness of
what the Lord expects of us and is to be respected.
Commitments of conscience must be kept. But our
consciousness is also part of us. And conscience, like
the rest of us, must be open to growth as we understand more and more what the commitment means.

If the priest is conscience in us, the congregation is
the crowd of our natural desires for the good things of
life. These too are good. But they can make mistakes if
they judge simply on the strength of each desire or
each experience of good as it comes. If feelings alone
make the judgment, they seem to want to take us over,
selling us into the service of whatever taste or lust
(or savior complex) we enjoy the most. Excited desires
can blind us to any other needs, just as they can
our children.

The sins of the priest and congregation concern
primarily the self and God. Those of the ruler and the
common people concern our relations with each
other. The ruler who directs the affairs of daily life in
the community symbolizes the principles of mutual

usefulness, while the ordinary citizen carries out the principles, applying them in particular instances. Unintentional errors can happen in either area, by mistaking the principles of good life or by misjudging the example. I may have lacked an adequate parent as a child and have no understanding of the principle of being a parent, of the amount of responsibility to take or of the times to exert authority, and so I may exert no overt authority at all over my child. I intend no harm. My mistake once identified can be corrected and forgiven. And yet harm does occur. Rulers as well as priests can make mistakes.

A sin of the common people is in the application of the principle. A new situation is precisely one not covered in any familiar way by principle. If I become a parent, I am faced with different modern authorities as well as with my memories of my mother or father. One expert shows that it is right to leave the child to "cry it out" and so learn to adjust to the reality and the schedule of those around. Another says to follow the timing of the child, feeding normally on demand until the infant is assured of his or her own identity and value as a person to be loved. Both principles have been taught. My mistake as citizen is not in desiring evil for a child, but in not knowing which principle to apply.

Experience itself can be confusing. I learn that I have different responsibilities in different roles. I may know the principle of what makes a good employee or manager of a business and the principle of what makes a good parent. But my child's event and my business appointment may coincide. My problem may be not in misunderstanding the principles, but in knowing how to apply them in a particular instance.

Four sources, then, of unintentional harm are distinguished—the priest, the congregation, the ruler, and the common people; in us, these represent the conscience, the feelings, the understanding of the principle, and the practical understanding of how to apply the principle. Each of these four areas is recognized and given its way to go to God for healing.

The way for the priest or for the congregation is the same. The offerer is to bring a bull, the symbol of the working strength of the natural mind, in this case perverted to the work of evil. The offerer (the priest himself or the elders acting for the congregation) as usual puts his hand on its head, identifying with the work as his, and then slaughters it himself, giving it entirely into God's hands. The blood is sprinkled seven times before the veil of the tabernacle—the veil, that is, between the commandments in the innermost tent of meeting and the outer court of our conscious sense of God's presence and our worship. The blood is the living thought, in this case in the state of repentance; sprinkling before the veil means turning the direction of the thought to be open to heaven and learning of God. The blood is then touched to the horns of the altar of incense in thankful perception of the sweet smell of forgiveness. The remainder of the blood is poured out at the base of the altar, the base that connects it to our common life; and the sacred inner parts and fat are burned on the altar exactly as they are for the peace offering. But now the rest of the bull is not eaten. It is taken, together with the skin and dung, outside the camp to a clean place and burned to ash. The way to freedom from the harm committed is not denial and attempts to forget it, nor war against it, nor eating it, swallowing it and living it until we no longer notice it because it is ourselves. The way is trusting God enough to go with it to God and then giving it out of our hands into God's, to be taken outside our living area to be burnt to ash.

The way for the ruler or for one of the people is the same, except that blood is touched to the horns of the altar of burnt offering, outside the tent, and that the animal is different—a male goat for the ruler, a female goat or sheep for one of the people. We have seen the male animal as the begetting principle and the female as the fruit or application of the principle, the goat as understanding and the sheep as loving. The ruler brings his or her male goat to the Lord, asking to be taught understanding of the principle. The people's error may be from a mistaken understanding of how to apply the principle or from a mistaken feeling of unwillingness to apply the principle in the case at hand. The people have the choice to make between the goat of understanding and the sheep of feeling.

These four sources of error with their different ways of turning to the Lord ask us to take seriously the interaction of the different parts of ourselves. Whose judgment has been at fault? Any one of our four parts, separated from its balance with the others, can lead to hurt. Who, then, calls them wrong? We do, as one whole person, when we see that something has gone wrong and have enough trust in the Lord and the integrity the Lord has given us to take a step toward change. The intent in the repeated detail is not to encourage us to feel sinful before God's judgment but to help us understand our inner process, to see where the problem lies and to get help.

The hurts we are concerned with here are all unwitting, coming from good intentions. And yet an immense amount of suffering can come from good intentions; children are injured by parents' mistaken kindness; we all have been dwarfed by mistakes of education; our social and civil relations in every direction are distorted by errors of principle and practice. It seems wrong that people are hurt by the mistakes of those on whom they depend. It is painful to discover that we have done an injury to someone dependent on us. But for us in the Western world, the solution is not to cut off all attachment to others. Our sense of growth toward our humanity demands relationships and choices with consequences, real joy in one another's wisdom and goodness, real pain in one another's faults. Only in such a context can good judgment, discerning good from evil, or helpful sympathy, have meaning.

The congregation is to bring its offering when its sin becomes known, and the ruler or any one of the people is to bring his when the sin which he has committed is made known to him. If, as human beings, we do affect each other and would not have it otherwise, the choice is not within our power to avoid the joy or hurt that is a part of all relationship. Our critical choice comes rather when it is made known to us that we have sinned. Sometimes at this point I deny the realization and continue as before, but now with the added pain of defensiveness, avoidance, and rationalization, with a new touchy area to carry along with me with great care. Sometimes I improve on the realization and change my overt behavior, but take on a destructive, hopeless guilt to use against myself, a new source of depression. And sometimes I accept the realization for what it is, a way of learning.

From experience, and after the event, I know that neither denial nor depression is worth the effort. But how can reading about the unwitting sin of priest, or congregation, or ruler, or people, be of help in making a better critical choice? How can it help me to accept the realization and to learn?

For one thing, it helps to be specific. To go to God with hurt or sadness in general, no matter how severe the hurt or sadness, can do more to reinforce than to relieve the problem. Regret on finding I have hurt another can be unbearable unless I ask for help. But to bring the regret of unintentional sin to God, I must bring the specific part of me that needs the healing— my conscience, feelings, understanding, or practicality. My attention has already shifted from the hopeless pain of guilt to the question that starts the learning: what went wrong? Was it the understanding, of conscience or of principle, that got separated from feeling and so became unreal? Was it feeling, left to run blind without the insight of reason, that lost perspective? Whichever it was, there is a way to put it in the Lord's hands and be healed. But first I need to bring the specific offering, and this itself is a decisive and essential change.

Even if, at this point, I don't yet know which part of me went wrong and need to ask the Lord for guidance, my asking is in a positive direction, and I am already breathing a different air, an air of hope.

For another thing, it helps to come off the dead center of my war against myself and take action. I must come to the Lord with my offering, conscious of the part of me that needs the healing, but conscious also of my power to take a decisive step as a person. I am no longer trapped in either a blind alley, of reasoning or of feeling only, overwhelmed by the guilt or pain that is all that I can see. I come, I who made the original choice, aware again of the two sides of my being, one whole person with perspective.

The Lord I know through the Bible is Truth itself and Love itself in the positive peace of Goodness itself, not one or the other, nor one against the other. The choice of the goat or sheep or of the male or female animals reminds me of the male and female sides in me, as in all people, the symbols of my truth and love, my understanding and my feeling. My peace is in the inner, peaceful marriage of these two parts of me, with neither one as tyrant or at war against the other. In *Conjugial Love* §65, Swedenborg states, "When love approaches wisdom or unites with it, then love becomes love; when wisdom in turn approaches love and unites with it, then wisdom becomes wisdom." Love and wisdom are not feelings operating without reason. They are not facts accumulated as knowledge apart from an intuitive human common sense. They are a unity of mutual respect. And when I turn to the Lord for help with one side or the other, I am conscious of the wholeness of a wiser love.

For a third thing, it helps to know that I am expected. Even when I love the Lord and try to love my neighbor, I am not always wise or loving. And so the ways are open for me to go to the Lord with the part of me that needs its healing. We are not asked to be always thinking of the Lord or always engaged in formal acts of worship. We are living human beings who do our work and make mistakes. We are asked to turn to the Lord to put ourselves in God's hands, to ask God's help, and learn and be forgiven. Our Lord knows our needs, has opened the way, and expects that we will come.

Why are there so many kinds of sin offering? Because the four basic parts of our learning edge—our conscience, feelings, reason, and practicality—all need our understanding. The Lord would not have us living on and on in unhappiness. We find the potential of the different parts of us by living them, not by keeping ourselves pure, apart from life. According to Swedenborg, even angels receive more loving ends and wiser love by similar processes of searching and return, for the joy the Lord would give is infinite in the deepening and discovery of that particular union of love and wisdom that is our inner self. When the ends or the ways we pursue bring grief, the Lord would have us come back, find the step that has gone wrong, learn what is good, and take that for our end with the Lord's peace and our wholeness in it.

· *Meditation* ·

Sit quietly for a moment. Feel your breath coming in and going out. Feel life moving in all parts of your body as they quietly and rightly work together. Rest for a moment in the goodness and the wholeness of being alive. Feel God's wisdom and power sustaining your life, giving life to every creature, sustaining the universe. Feel yourself quietly and rightly part of the wholeness, the goodness, and the wonder of life.

Let your mind turn to some feeling or thought that breaks that wholeness. Is it something you did that hurt another person? Something in you that is not right? Is it something you are ready now to bring to the Lord to be healed?

Is it something that touches your conscience? Your feelings for the good of life you want? Your ruler, trying to understand the principle of what you do? Or any ordinary citizen in you, not sure how to apply the principle to a particular case?

Whichever part of you it is, turn to it as a friend. Stretch out your hand and take its hand, knowing it as part of you with its power of conscience or feeling or understanding or practicality, and thank God for it. And now go to the altar of God, and give your sin offering totally into God's hands.

Reread Leviticus 4:1–12 to hear God's promise of the way of healing:

The LORD spoke to Moses, saying, Speak to the people of Israel, saying: When anyone sins unintentionally in any of the LORD's commandments about things not to be done, and does any one of them:

If it is the anointed priest who sins, thus bringing guilt on the people, he shall offer for the sin that he has committed a bull of the herd without blemish as a sin offering to the LORD. He shall bring the bull to the entrance of the tent of meeting before the LORD and lay his hand on the head of the bull; the bull shall be slaughtered before the LORD. The anointed priest shall take some of the blood of the bull and bring it into the tent of meeting. The priest shall dip his finger in the blood and sprinkle some of the blood seven times before the LORD in front of the curtain of the sanctuary. The priest shall put some of the blood on the horns of the altar of fragrant incense that is in the tent of meeting before the LORD; and the rest of the blood of the bull he shall pour out at the base of the altar of burnt offering, which is at the entrance of the tent of meeting. He shall remove all the fat from the bull of sin offering: the fat that covers the entrails and all the fat that is around the entrails; the two kidneys with the fat that is on them at the loins; and the appendage of the liver, which he shall remove with the kidneys, just as these are removed from the ox of the sacrifice of well-being. The priest shall turn them into smoke upon the altar of burnt offering. But the skin of the bull and all its flesh, as well as its head, its legs, its entrails, and its dung—all the rest of the bull— he shall carry out to a clean place outside the camp, to the ash heap, and shall burn it on a wood fire; at the ash heap it shall be burned.

Now visualize the priest in you, in that place of light outside the veil, bringing your offering to God, giving to God the source of your feelings and your memory, and taking the rest, skin and dung and all, outside the camp to a clean place and burning it to ash.

Lord, thank you that all I am and know and
think and feel, you know already,
and you still love me,
that even when I come apart and hurt others and
myself, you still love me, every part of me,
and give me life and bring me into being.
Thank you that you would have me be myself
and find my wholeness, my forgiveness, and my healing.
Thank you, Lord.
Amen.

10

When any of you sin in that you have heard a
public adjuration to testify and—though able
to testify as one who has seen or learned of the
matter—do not speak up, you are subject to
punishment. Or when any of you touch any
unclean thing—whether the carcass of an
unclean beast or the carcass of unclean livestock or the carcass of an unclean swarming
thing—and are unaware of it, you have become
unclean, and are guilty. Or when you touch
human uncleanness—any uncleanness by
which one can become unclean—and are
unaware of it, when you come to know it, you
shall be guilty. Or when any of you utter aloud
a rash oath for a bad or a good purpose, whatever people utter in an oath, and are unaware
of it, when you come to know it, you shall in
any of these be guilty. When you realize your
guilt in any of these, you shall confess the sin
you committed. And you shall bring to the
LORD, as your penalty for the sin that you have

committed, a female from the flock, a sheep or a goat, as a sin offering; and the priest shall make atonement on your behalf for your sin.

Sin offerings provided a way to deal with unintentional error caused by an imbalance within ourselves. They asked us to look inward to see the part of us that was malfunctioning and find our integrity as persons and our wholeness. Guilt offerings ask us to look outward to our relations with others as well as with God, to see the evil that comes to us from our society and the evil we do in our relationship to God or to our neighbor—in other words: defilement and transgression.

It would be delightful if we could go through the world untouched by the evil of it, having no memories of unclean acts or words to come unbidden, knowing only good. But who reaches even the first stages of adulthood without experience of evil? And who can stop here and say that he or she has not taken pleasure in some evil? We are not excluded from the world. And even if we were, exclusion would not result in purity of thought. It takes experience, including the involvement of the feelings and not just thought from afar, to produce positive hatred of evil as evil or real delight in goodness. Our task is not to avoid contact with the world, but to learn to know evil as evil, to know, that is, with feeling and by living, as well as by reasoning about it.

Our text begins with a strong statement on responsibility to bear witness and then goes on to deal with offerings for defilement. The courage to witness, to speak out and not let the thing remain hidden, is stressed in every instance of defilement. If anyone has seen evil and is called to testify as "one who has seen or learned of the matter" yet does not speak up, he is defiled. Seeing or knowing evil is not the problem, then, but failing to witness to it. But if that is true, why do I feel so filthy when I see evil done by others? I think the mischief is that those who do it, or those who report to me in horror about the ones who do it, take pleasure in it, and there is in me a capacity for similar pleasure. And so I go through an issue with myself. In the light of day, with its real quality clearly seen, the evil can do me little harm. But taken into the half darkness of the inner recesses of my mind, it is food to the animals there that love the darkness. Shall I just keep it there a little, before I really look at it, see clearly what it is, and face the knowledge that I too take pleasure in it?

This is the danger point, the non-decision that lets it be absorbed and shuts it up inside for secret pondering. When we know evil in our outer world and refuse to testify, we are accessories to it. When we keep any evil we have seen or heard in this state of half-knowing, concealing it from the light, we bear our iniquity. We keep it with us, a continuing source of uncleanness in our memory and thought. Defilement comes from outside. When it is left outside—evil recognized as evil—it can go by and leave no damage. But my fear of knowing that I enjoy the evil makes me invite it inside, and this is the problem. The fact is we do take pleasure. If we see that and see the thing as evil, evil enough to turn away from it, and say this before God and ourselves, we are free.

An evil seen or heard requires our witness, then. We must acknowledge it as such, and the same applies to any unclean thing we touch that may defile us. Israel knew clean and unclean animals. Clean domestic animals, clean cattle or sheep or goats or pigeons were eaten and also used for sacrifice, while wild or unclean animals were not. Wild deer and some other animals of the hunt were clean and could be eaten. No bird or beast of prey or weasel, mouse, or lizard, or swarming thing that crawled upon the earth, or animal that died of itself, could be sacrificed or eaten (Lev. 11 and Deut. 14). Unclean wild animals are symbols of the fierce passions, the desire to kill, to tear to pieces, to steal, to plunder, or, in the case of creeping things, to spy and gather in appearances of evil. Feelings that prey on other feelings or scavenge for the remains of old, dead feelings can be dangerous beyond all reasonable expectation. These animals we do not eat or bring for sacrifice. I think we all know the wolf and fox in us. The Bible speaks also, among other beasts, of hornets, vultures, leopards, lions, wild asses, poisonous snakes, and crocodiles. If we cannot avoid these realities and cannot sacrifice them, what do we do? Does just touching them make us unclean?

On this point, the text is clear. Touching them does not defile us. What does defile is touching their carcass and letting that be hidden.

Does that mean I can feel desire to kill and not be guilty? Isn't that what anger is? And isn't that why Jesus says that anger makes people "liable to judgment," just like murder?

Anger, as both the Hebrew and the New Testament recognize, can lead to murder. Anger is dangerous. But the Bible sees it as a part of life. There is a distinction between the person who is "slow to anger" and the one who is quick (Prov. 14:29 and elsewhere). Live anger felt and live anger channeled into violent action against others are also two different things. The Bible sees God's anger as the force of love ready to act against injustice to free persons from oppression (Ex. 22:24). Live anger channeled into acts of mercy is not evil. Anger gone sour or used as an excuse for violence is the problem. And Leviticus in our text distinguishes between the unclean animal and its carcass. What is the difference between live and dead anger? What does it mean to touch a living lion or a dead one? The lion can be the symbol of the power of good or of truth in power from good. God's blessing on Judah is that he will rule with the strength of a lion (Gen. 49:8–10). God will "protect and deliver" and "spare and rescue" Jerusalem "as a lion or a young lion growls over his prey" (Isa. 31:4–5). But lions, like other symbols, can have another side. They are destroyers who will make Israel's land a "waste" in Jeremiah 4:7.

God's love is the source of life. There is no other source. The power of the lion is blessed and alive as long as it is the force of a love that comes from God. Dead anger, cut off from spiritual life and kept alive artificially by my own power alone, to serve my ego and do violence, defiles. The wolf has good, quick power to seize, as well as ravenous swallowing up of stolen prey. The fox has excellent strategy, for good or ill. So every animal in the list has a positive and a negative power.

The power of anger is dangerous. So is the power of love. And to the extent I lack either power I know I am not real. And when I fear either power so much I keep it hidden, I find it later as a carcass. Dead animals of any kind symbolize feelings cut off from their real source. The willingness to touch the living power of any feeling and know openly its reality is the issue here. It is the dead wolf or fox or lion that we try to keep hidden or use as an excuse for doing violence that defiles.

Unclean animals are not the only problem. Contact with human uncleanness, awareness of the filthy thought of others, also has its effect on us. If we fall in with it, we feel unclean. If we do not, we may react too much and find our thoughts and words rushing tumultuously to commit us rashly to something we find we hate or to a good so absolute we know we cannot do it.

When we are affected by evil of any of these kinds, our first response is naturally to feel that the defilement is our own. And so, before we even clearly see it, we tend to hide it in ourselves and make it actually our own. At this point, awareness of the Word of God is crucial. The intent of every sin or guilt offering is forgiveness. No matter in what way defilement comes, the Lord does not impute the evil to us but wants us to be free of it. One of Swedenborg's most absolute and emphatic convictions is that "the Lord imputes good to every man" (*True Christianity* §650).

If God is Love itself and Mercy itself, and so Good itself, we cannot think that God would do evil to anyone. Swedenborg's experience with people in heaven and in hell convinced him that those in hell are those who impute evil. We all come in contact with enough evil: those voices that instantly suggest the added evil of "You are guilty" or "You are involved, with no way out" are voices of hell. When we listen to those voices and mistake the potential we have for pleasure in the evil of actual guilt and become frightened, we hide the unclean thing in ourselves and do make it our own. When we listen to God's Word and trust God's goodness, we can then look at the evil clearly and see the fierceness, the filthiness, or the violence present in our thoughts, and turn to God for help.

The guilt offerings, then, ask us not to take the evil into us, but to see the evil and then to see what good the evil is disrupting. Is it our living in mutual love that is upset, or our confidence in God's love for all, or our doing the thing we know is right? These things in us are displaced by filth. We are to bring the symbol of that good to God, a female goat or sheep (or, if these are not right for us, two pigeons or fine flour), identifying the evil that would harm it and asking the Lord to remove the evil from us and fill the gap with positive good. And so we bring the clean, domestic animal for our offering and not the wild one. The Lord asks us not to stand and feel how guilty we are, but to turn away from the evil thing and ask to have the space filled with good. This it is to be forgiven, free from defilement.

· *Meditation* ·

Be quiet. Turn your mind to God's amazing, consistent love for you. Rest quietly for a moment in God's goodness, the reality of all that is, that does no evil, the goodness that, no matter what feeling you have had, does not want you to be guilty, but wants your healing.

Read again Leviticus 5:1–6, and hear the Word of God to you that there is a way to come from the touch of any unclean thing to the Lord, to be free of it.

> When any of you sin in that you have heard a public adjuration to testify and—though able to testify as one who has seen or learned of the matter—do not speak up, you are subject to punishment. Or when any of you touch any unclean thing—whether the carcass of an unclean beast or the carcass of unclean livestock or the carcass of an unclean swarming thing—and are unaware of it, you have become unclean, and are guilty. Or when you touch human uncleanness—any uncleanness by which one can become unclean—and are unaware of it, when you come to know it, you shall be guilty. Or when any of you utter aloud a rash oath for a bad or a good purpose, whatever people utter in an oath, and are unaware of it, when you come to know it, you shall in any of these be guilty. When you realize your guilt in any of these, you shall confess the sin

you committed. And you shall bring to the
LORD, as your penalty for the sin that you have
committed, a female from the flock, a sheep or
a goat, as a sin offering; and the priest shall
make atonement on your behalf for your sin.

Now let your mind be open to the guilt or the
uneasiness that has been bothering you, and this time
don't turn away before you see it. Look at it. Is it some
feeling that you hate yourself for feeling? What feeling? Is it some evil you have seen someone do? What
was the evil in it? What feeling comes in you as you
think about it?

Look at your feeling. Is it a lust to kill? A dead body
of some anger? Some other unclean animal? Feel
again the touch of it, the filthiness, the fear, the desper-
ate need to run away. This time don't run, but turn and
see the Lord with you, caring for you, not looking
away, but asking you to come. Look again at that dead
body. And see it as it was alive. What was its strength
for you, that strength so strong you ran away from it
and never told yourself or God? See again that lion (or
whatever creature it is), alive and strong, and see it as
your friend. Reach out and touch it and feel its
strength beside you to help you, and feel your confidence. What was the good that was disrupted when
you ran away? A good of love, of strength of caring for
yourself or someone else? An insight into how to do
the loving or right thing? Now bring your lamb of
good or goat of insight to the Lord. And know the

Lord is there. And give your gift, with all its life, into the Lord's hands. Greet the priest in you, and give the source of your feelings and your memory of this thing to the altar, that they be for your good. See the priest in you take all the rest, skin and dung and all, outside the camp to be burned to ash. And now, again, be still a moment, and let new life come in.

Lord, thank you.
Thank you that I can trust you with myself, my hurt,
my fear, my guilt,
or any of the things I touch or feel or do, and that you
want my healing.
Thank you for healing me.
Amen.

11

· Guilt Offerings: Transgression ·
Leviticus 5:14–16; 6:1–7

The LORD spoke to Moses, saying: when any of
you commit a trespass and sin unintentionally
in any of the holy things of the LORD, you shall
bring, as your guilt offering to the LORD, a ram
without blemish from the flock, convertible
into silver by the sanctuary shekel; it is a guilt
offering. And you shall make restitution for
the holy thing in which you were remiss, and
shall add one-fifth to it and give it to the priest.
The priest shall make atonement on your
behalf with the ram of the guilt offering, and
you shall be forgiven. . . .

The LORD spoke to Moses, saying: When
any of you sin and commit a trespass against
the LORD by deceiving a neighbor in a matter
of a deposit or a pledge, or by robbery, or if you
have defrauded a neighbor, or have found
something lost and lied about it—if you swear
falsely regarding any of the various things that
one may do and sin thereby—when you have
sinned and realize your guilt, and would

restore what you took by robbery or by fraud or the deposit that was committed to you, or the lost thing that you found, or anything else about which you have sworn falsely, you shall repay the principal amount and shall add one-fifth to it. You shall pay it to its owner when you realize your guilt. And you shall bring to the priest, as your guilt offering to the LORD, a ram without blemish from the flock, or its equivalent, for a guilt offering. The priest shall make atonement on your behalf before the LORD, and you shall be forgiven for any of the things that one may do and incur guilt thereby.

*G*uilt offerings for defilement showed us the way to turn to God for healing of the unclean feelings that seem to appear in us from no deliberate intent of ours. As we encounter what is filthy in the world, we find the parts of us that understand the filth. We know our need for cleansing, although the occasion seems to come from circumstances outside ourselves. Now, finally, we come to our transgressions, the overt acts that we have done against our God or neighbor.

The first part of the text deals with transgressions committed unwittingly against God. We may commit a breach of faith and sin "unintentionally in any of the holy things of the LORD." These "holy things" include the giving of tithes or other offerings due to God, the symbol that all we have is a gift from God. The Lord loves all people tenderly and generously. There is no depth of affection the Lord would not give us to enrich our lives and no breadth of wisdom the Lord would not give us for our delight. The change of attitude that sees the presence of God's goodness not as a gift but as something we have done does, always, seem to be unwitting. The effort that is part of any spiritual growth appears mysteriously as credit in our ledger. Consciously we know that pride in truth received means loss of light, that good things done with reliance only on ourselves fail through lack of steady love or through complacency. But how much of God's grace can we receive without unconsciously shifting our position to one of bargaining or of deserving?

The Lord alone loves steadily, with majestic intensity, and at the same time with absolute modesty and respectfulness. The Lord alone, knowing all things, can value wisdom solely as a means of embodying love for others. It is not an arbitrary law that requires regular looking to the Lord for good and acknowledging the Lord in the good we receive; it is the principle of life. And the failure we experience when we do not look to the Lord is not an arbitrary penalty; it is the fact of life.

And so we are to bring silver shekels for the amount of tithe or offering withheld, adding an extra fifth, and a perfect ram from the flock for a guilt offering. Gold and silver are solid knowledge left with us by experience, gold by experience of the goodness of God, silver by experience of the truth. We bring silver, representing an intelligent knowledge of God's gift and of the mistake of crediting it to ourselves. The fifth is two tithes, symbols of all of the goods and truths from God stored up in our inner selves, to represent the full acknowledgment that God is the source of life. The flock is those who love and follow their Lord, and so the ram symbolizes an innocent desire to know God's will and do it. To bring this offering is to bring ourselves into the pattern of reality, to be open to the one source of all life and energy, so that we may live.

The second part of the text deals with the final kind of transgression, deliberately dealing falsely with our neighbor. This too is a trespass against the Lord, a sin against the Lord's love for all, as well as a trespass against our neighbor. The biblical tradition as a whole connects the love of God with love of neighbor. This is brought out clearly later in Leviticus 19 in that most sensitive treatment of what it means that God asks us to "be holy." The reason that "you shall love your neighbor as yourself" is not to gain reward, but that "I am the LORD" (Lev. 19:18). The reason that "you shall love [the stranger] as yourself" is that "you were aliens in the land of Egypt" and that "I am the LORD your God" (Lev. 19:34). Jesus makes the king in his parable say, "just as you did it to one of the least of these who are members of my family, you did it to me" (Mt. 25:40). Rabbis shortly before the time of Jesus similarly saw the quality of "singleness," of single-hearted devotion to the will of God alone, as inextricably bound up with charity to the neighbor (T. Issachar).

The breach against our neighbor is, then, against our God as well. It is a breach we can commit in many ways. We may deceive our neighbors in the matter of a trust accepted for material goods. We may deceive them at another level through our prejudice or dishonesty, preventing them from obtaining the truth or good that they desire. We may steal from our neighbors's material goods or by taking possession of their thoughts and affections and misusing them. We may betray a confidence. We may oppress our neighbors physically, either directly or by enjoying the benefit of labor inadequately compensated, or we may manipulate them psychologically, preventing freedom of thought and enjoyment. We may find what was lost and lie about it, twisting a situation for our benefit. We may swear falsely, promising what we know we may not do. We may injure our neighbors in a thousand different ways.

We cannot do these wrongs to others and not suffer from them ourselves, cutting ourselves off from the source of life and diminishing for all the trust and justice and charity that are abundant life. These wrongs are obvious injuries. We cannot easily plead innocent error. They are injuries we do to our neighbors. We cannot plead defilement coming from their sins or errors. Up to now, we could turn to God more or less confidently, with some reason to trust in mercy and with some excuse. We could, perhaps, identify the evil thing as evil and distinguish the evil action from ourselves who did or suffered it. But now, are we not faced with the fact that we are guilty? Should we not start, at least, to punish ourselves and so avert worse punishment to come?

This is perhaps the final test of our awareness of the facts of life. God's goodness is the source of life. There is no other. Good loves that do not feel natural to us, such as the love of truth or of loving others without regard to our own ego, are from God. They are given to us when we ask them from the Lord and use them as from the Lord. When we take them into our own hands to use apart from God, they lose their source of life. If we attempt to punish ourselves, to chasten ourselves to an unselfish love of truth, we may cut off some of the more obvious selfish motives, only to enlarge our deeper pride in our own intelligence or comprehensiveness; and then we have no clear light from God by which to discern truth from falsehood.

Self-punishment cuts us off from God. We let ourselves be fooled by hell's voice that we are guilty and that we have to deal with the evil ourselves before we dare to come to God. And so we fight in our own strength, without the source of all the strength there is, and lose.

Self-punishment serves hell, not heaven. "The Lord imputes good to every man and evil to none," wrote Emanuel Swedenborg in *True Christianity* §651.

God's constant love for every person is trustworthy. That steadfast love endures forever. It is a breach of faith against God when we are unfaithful to our neighbor. What heals the breach? We are to restore "the principal amount and shall add one-fifth to it" and "shall pay it to its owner," going first to our neighbor and doing our part to make it right with him or her. And then on the same day we are to bring a ram, a desire to know God's will and do it, to the priest, that our priest may make atonement for us before the Lord, so that we may "be forgiven for any of the things that one may do and incur guilt thereby." Again, we must identify the evil we have done and deal with it, not evading the specific by turning our attention to ourselves and feeling guilty.

Again the key point is that first awareness of the evil. That is the point at which we must trust God enough to look clearly at the evil in the light of God's presence and not run away and hide it somewhere in ourselves so we won't really have to see it and not try to fix it ourselves so that we never have to bring it to the Lord. Self-punishments, like dead lions, make us filthy. And God's will is for good, that we turn from the evil and to God and be free of it and live.

We are responsible to go to our neighbor, to restore "the principal amount and . . . add one-fifth," giving more than our original injury. Beyond this, we are not responsible. We are not the ones who make it right. We can only free our block, our defensiveness, so that the Lord's love will have the space to work for healing. It is not our judgment of the issue that solves the problem. And it is not we who go alone to bring about solution. It is God's mercy that goes, bearing us and our action with it as a kind of symbol of that love, if we but will. And the outcome, for ourselves and for the other, we must yield to God.

The way to deal with guilt is not denial, nor war against it, nor eating it. It is to put it in the Lord's hands, to be taken outside the camp and burned to ash.

Why are there guilt offerings? Not to convict us of guilt, but to free us from it. Removal of the evil and renewal of God's life in us are God's divine forgiveness. And so each offering, for sin, defilement, or transgression, ends with forgiveness. For the divine forgiveness is a sense of the Lord's love in us, of healing and of freedom to enjoying doing what is good and to perceive the ways of loving wisely.

· *Meditation* ·

Be quiet. Turn your mind to God's amazing, consistent love for you. Rest quietly for a moment in God's goodness, the reality of all that is, that does no evil, the utterly amazing goodness that, no matter what evil you have done, does not want you to be guilty but wants your healing.

Read again Leviticus 5:14–16 and 6:1–7, and hear the Word of God to you that there is a way to come back from any evil you have done, to the Lord, to be free of it:

> The LORD spoke to Moses, saying: when any of you commit a trespass and sin unintentionally in any of the holy things of the LORD, you shall bring, as your guilt offering to the LORD, a ram without blemish from the flock, convertible into silver by the sanctuary shekel; it is a guilt offering. And you shall make restitution for the holy thing in which you were remiss, and

shall add one-fifth to it and give it to the priest. The priest shall make atonement on your behalf with the ram of the guilt offering, and you shall be forgiven. . . .

The LORD spoke to Moses, saying: When any of you sin and commit a trespass against the LORD by deceiving a neighbor in a matter of a deposit or a pledge, or by robbery, or if you have defrauded a neighbor, or have found something lost and lied about it—if you swear falsely regarding any of the various things that one may do and sin thereby—when you have sinned and realize your guilt, and would restore what you took by robbery or by fraud or the deposit that was committed to you, or the lost thing that you found, or anything else about which you have sworn falsely, you shall repay the principal amount and shall add one-fifth to it. You shall pay it to its owner when you realize your guilt. And you shall bring to the priest, as your guilt offering to the LORD, a ram without blemish from the flock, or its equivalent, for a guilt offering. The priest shall make atonement on your behalf before the LORD, and you shall be forgiven for any of the things that one may do and incur guilt thereby.

And now let your mind be open to the evil you have done, and this time don't turn away. Look at it and see the evil of the thing you did. Who did you injure?

Mentally put that person into the Lord's hands to be comforted and feel the power of the Lord's compassion for him or her. And now, in the strength of that compassion, ask the Lord's help to know the pain you have caused and to know the way the Lord would want that person to be comforted.

Now put the evil and the pain, the other person, and yourself, into the Lord's hands. Whatever the action is you know that you will do, to go and see that person face to face and ask forgiveness, to make the phone call, to write the check or letter, to do your part to right the wrong, to see the Lord with you as you see what you will do. And see it not as a thing that you alone must do to stop the pain or heal the breach, but as an expression of your knowing that God's will is already moving with you both, with power to heal if you will let it.

Now whatever the good of love that was disrupted by your sin against your neighbor, see that good, and bring your ram of love and give it into the Lord's hands. Greet the priest in you, and give the source of your feelings and your memory of the evil to the fire of love upon the altar. See the priest in you take all the rest, skin and dung and all, outside the camp to be burned to ash. And now, again, be still a moment, and breathe deeply and gratefully, and let the good come in.

Lord, thank you.
Thank you that I can come to you and ask your help to
see the evil I have done
and turn from it, and live.
Help me to put myself, and my neighbor I have hurt,
into your hands.
Hold us, Lord, in your cleansing, healing love.
Thank you, Lord.
Amen.

Apocalypse Explained. 6 vols. Translated by John Whitehead. 2nd ed. West Chester, Pa.: The Swedenborg Foundation, 1994–1998.

Apocalypse Revealed. 2 vols. Translated by John Whitehead. 2nd ed. West Chester, Pa.: The Swedenborg Foundation, 1997.
   A new translation of this work, to be entitled *Revelation Unveiled*, will be available from the NEW CENTURY EDITION OF THE WORKS OF EMANUEL SWEDENBORG in the near future.

Arcana Coelestia. 12 vols. Translated by John Clowes. Revised by John F. Potts. 2nd ed. West Chester, Pa.: The Swedenborg Foundation, 1995–1998. The first volume of this work is also available under the title *Heavenly Secrets*.
   A new translation of this work, to be entitled *Secrets of Heaven*, will be available from the NEW CENTURY EDITION OF THE WORKS OF EMANUEL SWEDENBORG in the near future.

Charity: The Practice of Neighborliness. Translated by William F. Wunsch. Edited by William R. Woofenden. West Chester, Pa.: The Swedenborg Foundation, 1995.

Conjugial Love. Translated by Samuel S. Warren. Revised by Louis Tafel. 2nd ed. West Chester, Pa.: The Swedenborg Foundation, 1998. This volume is also available under the title *Love in Marriage*, translated by David Gladish, 1992.
   A new translation of this work, to be entitled *Marriage Love*, will be available from the THE NEW CENTURY EDITION OF THE WORKS OF EMANUEL SWEDENBORG in the near future.

Divine Love and Wisdom. Translated by John C. Ager. 2nd ed. West
   Chester, Pa.: The Swedenborg Foundation, 1995.

Divine Love and Wisdom/Divine Providence. Translated by George F.
   Dole. NEW CENTURY EDITION OF THE WORKS OF EMANUEL SWEDEN-
   BORG. West Chester, Pa.: The Swedenborg Foundation, 2003.

Divine Providence. Translated by William Wunsch. 2nd ed. West
   Chester, Pa.: The Swedenborg Foundation, 1996.

Four Doctrines. Translated by John F. Potts. 2nd ed. West Chester,
   Pa.: The Swedenborg Foundation, 1997.
   A new translation of the individual volumes of this collection—
   The Lord, Sacred Scripture, Life, and *Faith*—will be available from
   the NEW CENTURY EDITION OF THE WORKS OF EMANUEL
   SWEDENBORG in the near future.

Heaven and Hell. Translated by John C. Ager. 2nd ed. West Chester,
   Pa.: The Swedenborg Foundation, 1995.

————. Translated by George F. Dole. THE NEW CENTURY EDITION
   OF THE WORKS OF EMANUEL SWEDENBORG. West Chester, Pa.: The
   Swedenborg Foundation, 2000.

The Heavenly City. Translated by Lee Woofenden. West Chester, Pa.:
   The Swedenborg Foundation, 1993. See also *The New Jerusalem
   and Its Heavenly Doctrine*, below.

Journal of Dreams. Translated by J. J. G. Wilkinson. Introduction by Wilson Van Dusen. New York: The Swedenborg Foundation, 1986. See also *Swedenborg's Dream Diary*.

The Last Judgment in Retrospect. Translated by and edited by George F. Dole. West Chester, Pa.: The Swedenborg Foundation, 1996. See also *The Last Judgment and Babylon Destroyed*.

Miscellaneous Theological Works. Translated by John Whitehead. 2nd ed. West Chester, Pa.: The Swedenborg Foundation, 1996. This volume includes *The New Jerusalem and Its Heavenly Doctrine*, *Earths in the Universe*, and *The Last Judgment and Babylon Destroyed*, among others.

New translations of the individual titles in this collection will be available from the NEW CENTURY EDITION OF THE WORKS OF EMANUEL SWEDENBORG in the near future.

Posthumous Theological Works. 2 vols. Translated by John Whitehead. 2nd ed. West Chester, Pa.: The Swedenborg Foundation, 1996. These volumes include the autobiographical and theological extracts from Swedenborg's letters, *Additions to True Christian Religion*, *The Doctrine of Charity*, *The Precepts of the Decalogue*, and collected minor works, among others.

Swedenborg's Dream Diary. Edited by Lars Bergquist. Translated by Anders Hallengren. West Chester, Pa.: The Swedenborg Foundation, 2001. See also Journal of Dreams.

True Christian Religion. 2 vols. Translated by John C. Ager. 2nd ed. West Chester, Pa.: The Swedenborg Foundation, 1996.

True Christianity. 2 vols. Translated by Jonathan Rose. THE NEW CENTURY EDITION OF THE WORKS OF EMANUEL SWEDENBORG. West Chester, Pa.: The Swedenborg Foundation, forthcoming.

Worship and Love of God. Translated by Alfred H. Stroh and Frank Sewall. 2nd ed. West Chester, Pa.: The Swedenborg Foundation, 1996.

————. Translated by Stuart Shotwell. THE NEW CENTURY EDITION OF THE WORKS OF EMANUEL SWEDENBORG. West Chester, Pa.: The Swedenborg Foundation, forthcoming.

A Compendium of the Theological Writings of Emanuel Swedenborg.
Translated and edited by Samuel S. Warren. 1875; rpt. New York:
Swedenborg Foundation, 1974.

Conversations with Angels: What Swedenborg Heard in Heaven. Edited
by Leonard Fox and Donald Rose. Translated by David Gladish
and Jonathan Rose. West Chester, Pa.: Chrysalis Books, 1996.

Debates with Devils: What Swedenborg Heard in Hell. Edited by Donald
Rose. Translated by Lisa Hyatt Cooper. West Chester, Pa.:
Chrysalis Books, 2000.

Essential Swedenborg. Edited by Sig Synnestvedt. Rpt. West Chester,
Pa.: The Swedenborg Foundation, 1977.

Poems from Swedenborg. Edited by Leon C. Le Van. New York: The
Swedenborg Foundation, 1987.

A Thoughtful Soul. Translated by and edited by George F. Dole. West
Chester, Pa.: Chrysalis Books, 1995.

Way of Wisdom: Meditations on Love and Service. Edited by Grant R.
Schnarr and Erik J. Buss. West Chester, Pa.: Chrysalis Books, 1999.

Dr. Dorothea Harvey received her M.Div. at Union Theological Seminary and her Ph.D. in Literature of Religion at Columbia University. Now retired, she taught at Wellesley College, Milwaukee-Downer College, Lawrence University, and Urbana College. She is a minister in the Swedenborgian Church. Other publications by Dr. Harvey include works in the areas of literary forms, the prophets, forms of worship, and women in the Hebrew Bible.

Essential Swedenborg by Sig Synnestvedt
> A handy reference that presents the basic elements of Swedenborg's thought.

The Fashioning of Angels by Stephen and Robin Larsen
> A fascinating book that uses ancient wisdom to explore relationships.

Freedom and Evil by George F. Dole
> Examines questions about evil and hell from a Swedenborgian perspective.

Heaven in a Wild Flower by Vera Glenn
> Shares the meaning of growing things in a woman's life.

The Holy Center by Dorothea Harvey
> Uses biblical symbolism to explain how we can experience spiritual rebirth.

Johnny Appleseed, edited by William Ellery Jones
> Essays about the Swedenborgian John "Appleseed" Chapman.

Light in My Darkness by Helen Keller
> A beautifully written and inspiring revision of Keller's 1927 autobiography *My Religion*.

Lost Legacy, edited by Susan Poole
> Fascinating profiles of Swedenborgian women who challenged the conventions of their times.

The Presence of Other Worlds by Wilson Van Dusen
A fascinating account of Swedenborg's inner journey of the mind, with spiritual and psychological findings.

A Psychology of Spiritual Healing by Eugene Taylor
Integrates Western and Eastern thought into a holistic prescription for recovery and renewal.

Return to the Promised Land by Grant R. Schnarr
A practical twelve-step guide for spiritual recovery that employs a symbolic interpretation of the biblical Exodus to examine our own life crises.

Rooted in Spirit, edited by Alice B. Skinner
An anthology of writings by Swedenborgian women, in which the writers attest to the power of their heritage.

A Scientist Explores Spirit by George F. Dole and Robert H. Kirven
A lively, concise biography that introduces the life and spiritual thought of Emanuel Swedenborg.

Spirituality That Makes Sense by Douglas Taylor
A rational understanding of spiritual mysteries.

A Thoughtful Soul, edited and translated by George F. Dole
Selections from Swedenborg's writings presented as a series of thoughtful meditations.

Tunnel to Eternity by Leon Rhodes
Draws fascinating parallels between near-death experiences and the spiritual world described by Emanuel Swedenborg.

Way of Wisdom, edited by Grant R. Schnarr and Eric J. Buss
A collection of 100 quotations from Swedenborg, arranged for self-reflection and personal growth.

Visit us on the Web at <u>www.swedenborg.com</u> and "The Swedenborg Channel."